FILLING
A VOID

A RESOURCE FOR THE
JOURNEY TO MANHOOD

CHARLES D. DANGERFIELD

CD Dangerfield Enterprises
4801 Laguna Blvd., Suite 105, #380, Elk Grove CA 95758

charles@cdangerfield.com

This book is a work of non-fiction. Unless otherwise noted, the author and the publisher make no explicit guarantees as to the accuracy of the information contained in this book and in some cases, names of people and places have been altered to protect their privacy.

Scripture quotations taken from the New American Standard Bible® (NASB), Copyright © 1960, 1962, 1963, 1968, 1971, 1972, 1973, 1975, 1977, 1995 by The Lockman Foundation. Used by permission. www.Lockman.org

ISBN: 978-0-578-19476-9 (sc)
ISBN: 978-0-578-19477-6 (hc)
ISBN: 978-0-578-19478-3 (e)

Library of Congress Control Number: 2017918777

Because of the dynamic nature of the Internet, any web addresses or links contained in this book may have changed since publication and may no longer be valid. The views expressed in this work are solely those of the author and do not necessarily reflect the views of the publisher, and the publisher hereby disclaims any responsibility for them.

Image credit: Rudy Meyers Photography

Lulu Publishing Services rev. date: 12/02/2017

CONTENTS

Acknowledgments vii

Introduction ix

Chapter 1   My Story.. 1

Chapter 2   Choices, Decisions, and Consequences 15

Chapter 3   Identity.. 23

Chapter 4   Emotions 42

Chapter 5   Relationships 66

Chapter 6   Education and Knowledge.....................................101

Chapter 7   Employment and Finances.....................................114

Chapter 8   Leadership 135

Chapter 9   Social Issues 147

Chapter 10   Final Reflections 184

ACKNOWLEDGMENTS

As I travel the roads of my own journey, the more I understand and value the importance of others in my life. With that said, I need to take a couple of minutes to give some heartfelt thanks and shout-outs to a few people.

I will start with a huge thank you to my most amazing wife, Darlene "Lady Danger," for everything you do for me and our family, including being the first person to try to read through my "chicken scratch" as the book began to take form. Thanks to my "Momma Girl" for her strength and for setting me on the right path that has ultimately led to the writing of this book.

Thanks go out to Carletta, Chris, Victor, Cassie, Christina, James, Aunt Velma, Delonda, Kendall, and my peeps Darrell and Katrice for your time and extremely valuable input during the review process; to Mike and Maureen for your expertise and inspiration; to Sensei Tibon for always believing in me, and to my "grands" for understanding when I was holed up in the office for hours and days while working on this project.

A special thanks to my brothers from the youth and the law panels with whom I have been blessed to share not only the "stage" but the passion of "dropping knowledge" and giving back to untold numbers of young men. Thank you, Scott, Renard, Troy, Daniel, Michael, Rodney, Steve, Eric, and my "brotha" Ray for all you do.

Special shout-outs go to Jerry for your recommendation to provide real-life examples; to Jovon and Cynthia for telling me to give of my entire self in this book and to dig deep, "making it bleed"; and to Ms. Ann for your many hours of reviews and never-ending belief in the message of this book.

And saving the best for last, thank you to my heavenly Father for loving me enough to sacrifice your son Jesus so I don't ever have to be separated from you. And thank you for providing me with the life experiences and inspiration to write this book. To God be the glory.

INTRODUCTION

For as long as I can remember, I wished I had a father, or at the very least a positive male figure in my life—someone I could talk to, someone to explain to me exactly what it meant to be a man and how to become one. I feel my mother did an amazing job raising me. However, the one thing she could not teach me was how to be a man.

With the positive male figure void ever present in my life, I made many mistakes as I attempted to figure the whole "being a man thing" out on my own. Like me as a boy and a young man back then, innumerable black males are still trying to figure things out for themselves today. Unfortunately, in most black communities across America, there are huge voids of active fathers and positive male role models. What we don't have is a shortage of "baby daddies" and single black mothers doing the best they know how to raise black boys into good men. This void leads to black boys' guessing about how they are to act and carry themselves or being influenced by negative role models.

Prior to my retirement, I worked over twenty-eight years in law enforcement, beginning as a correctional officer in a prison within the California Department of Corrections (CDC). I also worked the streets of California's Bay Area, which includes the cities of Oakland and Richmond. I concluded my career as the chief of the CDC's Office of Correctional Safety (OCS), which is CDC's street law enforcement unit. During my career, I have witnessed much to support what I already knew, and that is that our communities are in dire need of positive men of color to step up and point these boys in the right direction to manhood.

With a strong sense of desire and responsibility to help "fill a void," I began to give thought to the idea of writing this book. My first thought was, *Who am I to be writing a book?* For years, I dismissed the idea, but for some reason, I started writing notes—notes with questions that I as a boy or young man without a positive role model would have loved to have been able to talk to someone about.

When I finally started to plan for the writing of this book, I soon realized it was nearly impossible to write a book that would cover everything that a young man needed for every situation. So I focused on topics that would provide a good foundation and, more importantly, make you think. I wrote this book with the mind-set that you and I are just sitting down talking, and I am sharing the many things I have learned along my own journey. With that said, although we are not face to face, I wrote this book with a more personal voice, utilizing terms like, "we talked" or "we discussed."

It is not my intention for this to be an in-your-face "this is what you'd better do" kind of book. It is more about providing information that a young man can have in the database of his mind to make him think and to hopefully make good, sound decisions. Since it is indeed your mind that governs your actions, it is imperative that you fill it with as much positive information as possible. At the heart of this book is the theme that life is about choices and decisions. You and only you will be the one held responsible and accountable for your actions. Sometimes these decisions are indeed life-altering; one seemingly simple decision can change your life path forever.

It is my hope that this book will be a resource to young black boys and men to think before they act. Society as a whole does not care to hear about your excuses for poor decisions. My hope is to remove the excuse "no one ever told me that" from all who read this book. I also believe it will be a resource for our single mothers and countless others looking for something to help our boys. Some of the subjects may be a little advanced for younger readers, but it is something tangible that they can come back to at different stages of their journey. At the very least, it should be a conduit to open up dialogue and get people talking about matters that they may take for granted or may have never thought of before.

As you read this book, you will intermittently see selected Bible scriptures between sections and chapters. I use these scriptures to help me reiterate some of the thoughts discussed. The majority of the scriptures come from the book of Proverbs. I have always been drawn to the wisdom and powerful words of Proverbs, I think because it has the feel of a father sharing knowledge, wisdom, and life lessons with his son.

Most of Proverbs is written by King Solomon, the son of King David (the same David that killed the giant with a sling and a stone). It is said that Solomon was one of the wisest men to have ever lived. I do not dare compare myself to King Solomon, but in the same spirit in which he desired to share wisdom and knowledge with others, I attempt to do with you. It is truly a blessing to me to have this opportunity to consider the many things I have learned on my own journey and share them with you.

It is also not my intent for this book to be preachy or to push my religious beliefs on anyone. However, as I started writing, I found it impossible to write this book without mentioning and sharing the knowledge, understanding, and wisdom given to me by my Lord and Savior Jesus Christ. Just as you may not agree with all the advice in this book, please don't let your thoughts and feelings toward Christianity stop you from reading and receiving something from this book. Last, I wrote this book from a lifetime of my experiences, observations, and perspectives as the black boy I once was and now as the black man I have become.

> "Commit your works to the Lord, and your plans will be established."
>
> —*Proverbs 16:3*

CHAPTER 1

MY STORY

This book is not about me. In fact, it really is all about you. I am merely here to try to help you on your journey to manhood. However, in order for you to understand where I am coming from, this first chapter will give you a little insight into who I am.

Growing up, I never really knew my father. My mother never tried to keep me from knowing who he was; it's just that he was never around due to drug addiction and incarceration. When I got older, I tried to establish a relationship, but by then it was awkward at best. For example, I had no idea what to call the man. If I needed his attention, I just made sure he could see me so that I wouldn't have to call him by his name, which was contrary to how my mom raised me. Calling him *Dad* just wasn't going to happen. To me, that is an earned title, not automatically given just because of conception. Although my father wasn't around when I needed him, there is one encounter with him that I believe set me in the direction I would go later. Often in life, the most valuable lessons come from negative situations. If you can see through the negativity, there is knowledge to be gained, but you have to open your eyes and see it for what it is.

When I was nine years old, my stepmother took me to visit my father, who was doing time in California's infamous Folsom State Prison. There are certain things that happen in your life that stay with you forever, and visiting my father in that place was one of them. How you choose to deal with these things are up to you. Folsom is the second-oldest prison in California. With its granite walls, guards in gun towers, razor wire, and castle-like appearance, it can be extremely intimidating to a young boy—perhaps even more so when the person you are there to visit is a stranger. After having been processed inside, seeing the bars, and hearing the slamming of gates, I finally saw my father being escorted toward us. He was wearing standard prison blues and had a humongous afro, which was quite fashionable in the 1970s when I visited him. I remember telling myself right then and there that I would never allow this to happen to me. Unfortunately, this scenario is not unfamiliar to many black children across the nation. This just happens to be one man's story—my story and the lessons I have learned along my journey.

My mother grew up extremely hard, often being forced to live in foster homes and girls' schools. She had me when she was seventeen years old. She has often told me that I was the first man she wasn't afraid to love. She also told me that she grew up not knowing what a good man looked like because she had never seen one. I am the oldest of her four children. My sister and two brothers have the same father, so my mother gave me their father's last name. That way we would all have the same last name. I will say that the Dangerfield name did come in handy in the future. After all, it's not easy to forget a name like that.

My mother was the difference maker in my life. By having me so young, she became another single black mother, a child herself trying to raise a child alone. Mama was and is an amazingly strong woman, not because she wanted to be but because she had to be. She had to be strong to survive or else cease to exist. Unfortunately, this is another common reality in our communities. It was my mother who instilled in me values, morals, and the importance of being a person of high character, regardless of how much money I made. It was through this lady that I got a firsthand view of a true work ethic. She sometimes worked two jobs if that was what it took to take care of her babies, even if it meant working as a maid and cleaning the homes of others.

Soon after I was born, Mom married my stepfather. She would officially be married to this man for many years. However, I can't ever remember him being around or living with us for more than a week at a time. I don't say that to complain, as life was much better when he was not around. While my stepfather was many things, *Dad* was not one of them. So the positive role model that I sought surely could not be found in Mr. Dangerfield. When he was around, there would be peace for a day or two; then the drinking would begin and the violence would start, but rarely toward us kids. The fights between him and Mom were horrific for any child to witness. In the neighborhoods I grew up in, when parents fought, it wasn't just a little argument with voices raised. Yes, voices were raised, but so were guns, knives, or whatever they could get their hands on.

On many occasions, the police had to be called, and sometimes someone had to go to jail. As I said earlier, Mom was a strong lady for sure, and my stepfather might have raised his hand to hit her, but he knew there would be hell to pay for that action. Back in the day, my mom had one of those heavy old cars—I think it was a Catalina. I will never forget the time when she chased after my stepfather with that car. I can't remember the exact reason they were fighting, but it resulted in his getting two broken legs when she ran him over with that beast of a car.

Again, I decided to take a negative situation and make it into a positive. While it wasn't possible for my stepfather to provide the example I was looking for, he indirectly taught me a valuable lesson that would stay with me the rest of my life. It's what I call the reverse role model. I decided that if I did the opposite of everything this man did, then I would have a chance of being a good man.

For most of my youth, we were on welfare, receiving aid from the county. I distinctly remember that before we were able to receive food stamps, Mom would bring home boxes of government-issued food items such as canned meat, powdered eggs, powdered milk, and of course the large blocks of government cheese. We were actually happy when we finally got food stamps. However, due to youthful pride, I hated having to bust out the food stamps at checkout lines. I quickly learned to strategically pick out the fastest lines, and I made sure none of my friends ever saw me pay with food stamps.

Mom always tried to better herself and the living conditions of her children. She was never content to continue receiving aid. She was so happy when she landed a good state job that allowed her to become independent for the first time in her life. I remember my mother's so-called friends calling her a fool for wanting to go to work instead of sitting back and getting "free money." Mom not only talked to us about hard work but also demonstrated it. This is just one of her many attributes that have stuck with me throughout my life.

Although my mother did a great job raising us against tremendous odds, there comes a time in a young boy's life when he needs to learn from a male what it means to be a man. No matter how strong a black woman is, the one thing she can't teach a boy is how to be a man. Now, please don't misunderstand me—not only did I respect Mom, but I feared her as well. She was greatly aware of the void in the lives of her boys that forced her to wear the hats of both Mom and Dad. I remember one time—I was probably around seven—when I saw this toy watch that I thought I just absolutely had to have. The problem was that I didn't have any money, so I decided to just take it. Big mistake! Of course I got caught, and when I got home, I was punished. There was no such thing as time-out back then in a black household. Mom proceeded to whip my butt while at the same time telling me all about the evils of stealing. Apparently she got tired, so she took a cigarette break and then came back to the lesson at hand. Let's just say the lesson stuck.

While that lesson did stop me from pursuing my shoplifting career, young boys eventually have to explore for themselves, and this is where the male-role-model void is magnified. The teenage years are difficult enough by themselves, but they become even more complicated when boys are trying to figure out on their own what it means to be a man.

Although I had an extremely tough mother and the desire not to end up in prison like my father, I was still a far cry from being a choirboy. I grew up on the south side of Stockton. While I was not a true thug because I refused to be a criminal, I did identify and hang out with the thuggish crowd. I dressed like them and went to the same parties, but when it came time to commit a crime, they knew to drop me off. I would see them later when it came time to chase the girls. Some called me scary or punk, but I didn't care. I just called it wanting not to go jail. I'm not saying it was easy saying no to peer pressure, but it was easier than ending up in that place I had seen my father several years back.

Most of my high school years were more about hanging out with the cool dudes and chasing females than they were about showing up and learning something. When I was fourteen, I managed to get a job at Kentucky Fried Chicken and stayed there for almost five years. I guess I started to think I was a man because I had a job and was making my own money, and I didn't have to bother my mother for the things I thought I needed. Mom had to work so she couldn't keep an eye on us like she would have liked. I remember when I bought my first car. Mom had allowed it since I was working. So one particular semester I was feeling extremely "mannish." I thought since I was working, had my car, and the girls told me I was cute, I could do whatever I wanted. I would find out just how wrong I was.

At the end of that semester, things would change dramatically. Apparently Mom and the school not only expected me to show up to school, but they also wanted me to study and get good grades too. However, when report cards came out, and I had gotten five F's and one D. Needless to say, Mom was not pleased. She told me that she was going to take my car. Thinking I was a man now, I reminded her that she couldn't do that because I had paid for that car out of my pocket. So she simply took the keys and dared me to say another thing, which of course I didn't. Back on the city bus line I went. I don't recall any girls telling me how cute I was while I was riding the bus. The loss of my car was the culmination of some really bad decisions I was making during that time. One of those poor decisions came when Mom got stranded due to a blown tire, so she called me to help. I had partied extremely hard that day, so when she called me to come get her, I asked her if she could get someone else to help her because I was tired. She calmly said, "Okay" and hung up the phone, and I went back to sleep. That particular night's sleep was anything but peaceful. I was violently awakened by this crazy black woman. She sat on my chest and beat me like a mixed martial artist long before there was such a thing as the *Ultimate Fighting Championship*. While the attack did indeed hurt, the idea of my leaving her stranded like that hurt so much more.

I was also messing up big time on my job. I was showing up late or not showing up at all. The boss put me on notice and told me that I had better get right or I would be gone. I definitely couldn't afford to lose my only source of income. In my senior year of high school, I finally decided that I wanted to get my diploma and graduate. That's when I stopped hanging around the party people, and I began acting like I wanted my job and an education. Since my grades were less than stellar, I had to do some serious scrambling to get extra units. I just managed to walk across the stage and get my diploma. In my family, that was a really big accomplishment; it just didn't happen in our family. Graduating from high school was the highest goal ever talked about. College was never mentioned because that is what white kids did, not black boys from the south side. The sad thing about high school was that my performance had nothing to do with its being too hard; I simply didn't apply myself. I thought I was a man and had it all figured out. Once again, the "void" reared its ugly head.

Also around the same time I started to wise up and open my eyes, I officially got involved in martial arts. I say *officially* because when I was around eight or so, my friend had invited me to go to the drive-in with his family. That is where I saw my first Bruce Lee movie, and I was hooked. Some of my friends had taken formal karate lessons and would come home from practice and try their new moves out on me. When I got old enough and could afford it myself, I started taking formal lessons in various forms of martial arts. It helped me become more focused and introduced me to real discipline. Martial arts would play a huge role in my life. Later, I earned my black belt in the Okinawan form of Karate-Do, called Goju-Ryu. Subsequently, I was also inducted into the Masters Martial Arts Hall of Fame.

When I graduated from high school, I was the assistant manager at KFC and was doing very well. My mother's demonstration of hard work had manifested itself in me and in my sister as well, who also worked at KFC. She stayed a lot longer than I did and would become one of the highest-ranking black women in the KFC Corporation. KFC had big plans for me to become a manager and run my own store, but I had other plans. While the money would have been really good, I felt I needed to get away from Stockton before I became trapped. So I decided I was going to go into the navy.

It really was ironic that I went into the navy. Earlier in high school, I had actually been in the Navy Jr. Reserve Officer Training Corps (NJROTC) for a while. I was the Junior Commander, but one of the requirements was that I had to wear a navy officer uniform to school once a week. Unfortunately for me, this was right around the time that I became ultra-cool and could not be seen around the school in a uniform. I also thought, *Why should I stay in this class? If I ever did decide to go into the military, it sure as heck isn't going to be on a ship in the middle of some ocean.* Again, I was wrong and could have used some real manly guidance on that decision. Going into the navy was one of the best decisions I ever made because it gave me structure and discipline. Before I went in, some folks told me that the military was no place for black boys. They asked me, "Why would you risk your life for a country that does not care about you?" I didn't see it that way. First of all, I saw it as a way to get away from Stockton and learn how to be a man. Second, I thought, *Why should only the white boys serve? This is my country too.* It may not be perfect, but I soon learned from my travels that I have never seen anyplace better, despite its imperfections.

In the navy, I was forced to grow up quickly. It taught me from day one that I am responsible and accountable for my actions. It also taught me that the world was so much bigger than just Stockton, California. Soon after boot camp, I could have used some manly guidance to avoid another big mistake. I got married, and my son was born on the military base. I'll share much more on this later, but for now I will say that the void got me again. I had no business getting married that young, nor did I have a clue what I should be looking for in a wife. Youth, raging hormones, and ignorance are a deadly combination.

After nearly four years of service in the navy, it was time to either reenlist or take my honorable discharge and move on, which is what I did. The navy was extremely good for me, but I felt that if I reenlisted, I would end up staying for twenty years, which is not what I wanted to do. I knew I wanted to be in law enforcement. In 1986, I got out of the navy, which was pretty scary. Not only did I not have a job, I now had a young family to take care of. I started submitting applications for law enforcement positions before I got out. Since I had a family to support, I didn't have the luxury of being picky, so I went with the first one to call me.

At the end of 1986, I got a call from the California Department of Corrections (CDC)—yes, the same department that I had spent my whole life trying to avoid. However, since I would be on the other side of the bars and was in dire need of a job, I decided to listen to what they had to say. When CDC called, I was again living in Stockton but now with my young family. The caller asked me if I would accept a position at Deuel Vocational Institution (DVI). I responded, "Where in the heck is that?" I was told it was in Tracy, California. Well, I didn't know anything about DVI, but I did know that Tracy was a thirty-minute drive from Stockton. So I accepted and was on my way to the academy a few months later. After six weeks at the CDC training academy, I headed off to DVI, and I would be lying if I said I wasn't at least a little scared.

Not only was it ironic that I was going to work in a prison, but I later would find out that my father had done time at DVI years before my arrival—just another example of life not going according to plan. Over the years, I have finally learned to let God direct my path because every time I tried to take the helm and steer the ship, I ended up lost or shipwrecked. I also learned to control the things I can and prepare my best for everything else. You cannot plan for everything life has in store for you, but you can control your actions and how you respond. I did not have to see my father at DVI. However, while I worked there, I saw plenty of people I had grown up around in Stockton, including my brother and other family members.

So there I was, twenty-three years old, fresh out of the navy, and working in one of California's fifteen prisons. By the way, that number had doubled by the time I retired. Prison can be a pretty intimidating place even to those who get to go home at the end of the day. Just think about it: you watch the news and hear about the evil things people do to one another. Then these people are put in one place when they are arrested and convicted. You can only imagine the negativity festering in these places. Not everyone locked up is evil, but they were convicted of felonies for which a judge deemed it necessary to separate them from society.

Just because these men go to prison does not mean they stop committing crimes or stop being who they are. Some do in fact learn from their mistakes and change for the better. However, if the court gave them a life sentence without the possibility of parole, it doesn't make a difference how much they change for the good because they are never getting out of prison. They could learn to float on air and receive sainthood from the pope, but if the judge gave them the big "LWOP" (Life Without the Possibility of Parole), the only way they would leave prison would be in a coffin or after a miracle sentence reversal.

I worked at CDC for over twenty-eight years, with twelve of those years being behind the walls of DVI. Over time, out of pure self-preservation, I learned to adapt to the violence and focus on not becoming a victim myself. Inside the prison, the correctional staff is the law, or "police," as the inmates called us. We, in uniform, represented all the things that put them there. So needless to say, the inmates not only preyed on other, weaker inmates but also on the folks who wore badges. Therefore, we could not be caught less than alert, or "slipping" as it is sometimes called inside. That job is definitely not for everyone.

One of the things that blew my mind when I went to work at the prison was that so many of the inmates had the same color skin as mine. I talked to a lot of inmates during my time and learned that not all of them were pure evil; there were a lot of similarities in our stories. What separated us was the life decisions we had made. Some had made many mistakes that led them on the path to prison. Some of them had made only one extremely serious bad decision. Sometimes the decision was committing a particular crime or just being with the wrong people at the wrong time. Some of these people would spend the rest of their lives regretting one bad decision. The evil ones spent their sentences not regretting their actions but simply regretting the fact that they got caught. Life is indeed too volatile and fragile not to seriously consider the consequences (get used to that word because you will be seeing a lot of it in this book) of your actions.

During my time at DVI, I was promoted to sergeant and lieutenant. In 1999, I left the prison and was promoted to the rank of special agent. I was still in CDC but no longer assigned to a prison. I began working as an investigator with the Office of Internal Affairs (OIA). Over the years, as CDC grew tremendously in size, the need for a unit outside of the institutions that investigated misconduct of staff became apparent. My initial assignment was as a member of the Deadly Force Investigation Team (DFIT) in Sacramento. DFIT's responsibility was to investigate anytime a CDC staff member used deadly force, including the use of firearms.

Working in the institution had been a great experience for me, and I was blessed with a lot of amazing opportunities. I learned early on that the only unit within CDC that was responsible for actually going after bad guys on the streets was the CDC's Special Service Unit (SSU). I was told I had to be at the captain level to even be considered. When I heard that, it became my career goal and the reason I first sought out to promote within CDC. The chances of making it to SSU were extremely slim since there were fewer than thirty such positions in the entire state. But finally, after more than four years as a special agent within the OIA, in 2003 I finally got my chance to do the assignment I had worked toward for most of my career.

SSU is one of six branches of the Office of Correctional Safety (OCS). It has five primary offices throughout California, and I was assigned to work out of the Bay Area, with its office at the time being in downtown Oakland. The office would later move to Richmond. A total of five special agents and one senior special agent (supervisor) were assigned to this office. It was our responsibility to support all prisons, fire camps, and parole units in the region. The region went from the Monterey Peninsula all the way up the coast to the Oregon border.

To support the prisons, we assisted them in complex investigations that started in the prisons and reached out to the streets or with drug and other contraband coming into the prisons. Also, priority calls came to us in the event of an escape from the prisons and fire camps in our region. That meant, stop whatever you are doing and report *now*. I cannot even begin to remember the number of escapes we investigated over the years. Those calls always seemed to come right after I had just managed to fall asleep. Often, the next chance to sleep wouldn't be for more than twenty-four hours. As SSU special agents, we were never truly off, but we knew that when we signed up for the job. Another crucial role of SSU special agents was to work closely with other federal, state, and local law enforcement agencies within our region, including the San Francisco, Oakland, Richmond, San Jose, and Salinas police departments. We also worked closely with the Federal Bureau of Investigation, Drug Enforcement Agency, State of California Department of Justice, and countless other cities and agencies. If there was a prison or parole nexus of ongoing criminal activity, we would get a call to assist in some high-profile cases.

As an SSU special agent, I was assigned to work with the agencies in the Richmond area. Richmond is a predominantly black and Hispanic community. It is a city like many others with hard-working folks doing the best they can with what little they have. It also has a long history of violence and gang activity. While I was working the streets of Richmond, I witnessed the results of violence. Unfortunately, more times than not, it involved blacks killing other blacks, usually for relatively minor reasons. Again, the cycle of violence was ongoing. We would often find that it was generational violence that had been going on for so long that most of those who were presently involved had no idea why they warred with the perceived enemy. When asked why they shot someone, they would say in a matter-of-fact manner something like, "They from Central, and we from the North." As a black man it was really sad to see. I think what hurt the most was seeing how young the shooters and victims were. It was sad because they thought that was what it took to prove their manhood.

I recall being on a team assigned to serve an arrest-search warrant on a homicide suspect. The serving of a search warrant is a very stressful event for all involved. It is even more so in the case of the service of a homicide warrant compared to, say, the service of a warrant looking for stolen property. So needless to say, when you hit a house as a member of a homicide warrant team, you had better be prepared because the person you are looking for has already proven that he or she has no problem taking a life. On this particular day, we lined up to serve the warrant and made entry with guns drawn. As we did, we gave loud orders for people to show their hands. We encountered a young black boy who was no older than eight, sitting on the couch watching cartoons. Barely looking up, the young man calmly said, "Oh, you guys are looking for my brother. He's not here. His chick already picked him up." What was disturbing was the fact that what normally would have been a very traumatic event for a boy was so commonplace to this one. It didn't even interrupt his television time. As we were leaving the apartment and getting into the van, several kids about the same age approached us and proceeded to tell us accurately exactly what type of firearms each of us carrying.

After approximately six years on the streets of Richmond, I was promoted to senior special agent, becoming the supervisor of the same unit in which I had worked as a special agent. It took a little adjustment to being a supervisor and doing paperwork. I was extremely blessed to have a really good group of guys working with me.

After serving in the supervisor role for several years, I was getting ready to retire in the latter part of 2013—or at least I thought I was. About two months before I was to leave, I received a call from the recently retired chief of OCS telling me that the undersecretary of all of the CDC (the number-two person in the entire department) wanted to talk to me. Now understand, I was a field supervisor in Richmond, which insulated me from the politics at headquarters in Sacramento, so my first question was of course, "Talk to me about what?" The ex-chief told me, "About being chief." Still lost in this discussion, I replied, "Chief of what?" When he told me, "The chief of OCS," I was in a total state of shock, and for a few seconds I said absolutely nothing as that sunk in. When I snapped out of shock and started to speak, all I heard coming out of my mouth were excuses why I couldn't do that job. I will admit, the excuses were purely driven out of unadulterated fear—fear of the unknown and operating outside of my comfort zone.

My reasoning was that I would go from being a field guy, chasing bad guys, to being a suit-wearing, meeting-attending, policy-making guy at CDC headquarters in downtown Sacramento. Not to mention that I would be jumping three promotional positions, which was simply unheard of. Last, I was planning to retire in two months. The retired chief listened to all of my excuses and then concluded by saying that the undersecretary still wanted to talk to me the following week. Since it was a Friday, I told him I would get back to him after the weekend. After I hung up the phone, I just sat in my vehicle as all of this sank in. I eventually called my wife and told her what had just happened. She was ecstatic because she had been telling me for years that I should be at headquarters as a decision maker. Apparently, she thought I was just talking about moving one position up, but when I explained to her I was talking about the chief position, she lost her tongue like I initially had—and trust me, that didn't happen often for her.

Over that weekend, my wife and I talked a lot, and I did a lot of praying. When Monday rolled around, I told the ex-chief to go ahead and set up the meeting. Advice I had often given other people was coming back to haunt me in a big way. You see, I always talked about what an honor it was to be a part of SSU and OCS, and I told people that, no matter what they did in life, they shouldn't let the reason they didn't try something be fear alone. So this was the ultimate test for me to put up or shut up. By the time the big meeting rolled around, I had changed my viewpoint. I was still undoubtedly scared of the immense step I was considering, but I now started to ask myself, *Why not me?* If it is meant to be, then it is God's will, and if He put me in it, He would carry me through it. After several meetings and surprise interviews, I eventually found myself at the state capital to be interviewed by the special assistant to Governor Brown. I was later appointed by Governor Brown and took over as chief of OCS for the State of California.

This was the biggest challenge of my career as there was so much to learn in a short amount of time. So I personified the term "hit the floor running." The first thing I did was try to get everyone to put OCS's and CDC's mission ahead of their own agendas. OCS's mission in part was, "To protect the public and serve the investigative and security interest of CDC." There was an initial push back because change does not come easily, particularly for people with type A personalities who work in OCS. I held my ground, and we collectively started heading in the same direction. Trust me, there were a lot of prayers and sleepless nights in that job. I was so blessed for the opportunity to lead such an amazing group of people.

I learned so much during this challenge. Before I even took the job, I learned that I could never be sure who was watching me. So I just assumed I was always being watched. In cases like that, if you carry yourself with true character and integrity, you will have nothing to worry about—a valuable lesson indeed. Second, I learned not to sell myself short, stay humble, and believe in who I was. Last, I learned the importance of having a strong hand to hold when the challenges of life knock on the door. My wife is an incredible woman; I am a blessed man indeed.

Throughout my life, I have certainly made many mistakes along the way. I cannot undo any of those mistakes now. I decided long ago that I would not let my mistakes define who I am. I've embraced those mistakes as life lessons, and I do my very best not to repeat them. As long as you live, you will make mistakes. Hopefully, you learn from them. If you don't, all you will get from the experience is the hurt and pain without the knowledge of what not to do in the future. Not only do I gather valuable knowledge from my mistakes, I feel I am compelled to share what I have learned with others in hopes that they can learn from my mistakes without having to endure the same headaches and heartaches.

I could take all the credit for my successes in life, but that would be a lie. I am nothing special—just a man with a God-driven, pressing need in my heart to share some of the things I wished someone would have shared with me when I was growing up. I am convinced—and no one could convince me otherwise—that my God has led my path. As my mother once told me, "His fingerprints are all over you." Just as I had to overcome my fear regarding being chief, I had to overcome my fear in writing this book. I have concluded it is my responsibility to share what I know, so "Why not me?"

"Trust in the Lord with all your heart, and lean not on your own understanding. In all your ways acknowledge Him, and He will make your paths straight."

—*Proverbs 3:5–6*

2

CHOICES, DECISIONS, AND CONSEQUENCES

Throughout this book, we will be discussing many topics. However, the foundation of this book is the importance of making well-thought-out choices and decisions. It is important that we establish the foundation from the start as it is relative to everything else we discuss in this book. Expect to hear the theme "make good choices and decisions" a lot. Now that I am older, I understand that in order to have a successful journey to manhood, it is imperative that your good choices and decisions greatly outnumber the bad ones. I can't speak on the subject of manhood without talking about the value of making good choices and the reality of dealing with negative consequences when you make poor decisions. During my journey, I have found that you must acknowledge, embrace, and put into action the concept that your choices and decisions indeed define your life. I would even go so far as to say that it is *impossible* to be the best man you can be without fully embracing this concept.

We are going to start this chapter off with a few definitions. I want to ensure that we are all on the same page. The first one is for the word *choices,* which is defined as "the act of choosing; selection, the right, power, or chance to choose; option." Next, we have *decision*, which is "the act of making up one's mind; a conclusion reached or given." The last one for right now is *consequence*," and it is defined as "a result of an action, process, outcome, effect." Based on these definitions, if I have a *choice* between touching the flame on the stove and simply turning it off and I *decide* to touch it, then the obvious result or *consequence* is that I will get burned. Yes, this is an overly simplified yet appropriate example. If you choose to play with fire and decide to touch it, the consequence is getting burned.

I cannot stress enough the importance of understanding these three words. Perhaps they appear simple by themselves, as individual words, but collectively they establish the concept we need to lock in our brains right now and utilize every day for the rest of our lives. Since we are in school mode, let's stay in class and do a simple math equation. Even my silly class-cutting butt knows that one number plus another number equals the sum of those two numbers, like 1 + 1 = 2. So let's use that model equation to demonstrate that poor choices (PC) plus bad decisions (BD) equal negative consequences (NC): PC + BD = NC. We will simply refer to this as "the equation" for short.

One of the problems I saw in myself and others when I was growing up was that we failed to understand just how important this equation really is. I think we understand the meanings of these words individually, but we can totally miss the mark if we don't understand how they go hand in hand. We must take them collectively, as a whole, and in their totality. Just as 1 + 0 does not equal 2, poor choices plus bad decisions will not result in positive consequences.

It is extremely important that you embrace and incorporate the PC + BD = NC equation concept starting right now. You are never too young or too old to start making good decisions. You can tell yourself that you have no idea how you ended up in a particular situation or consequence. You can even tell yourself and others that somehow you just ended up in the consequence portion of the equation without going through the choice or decision-making part. I am here to tell you that's just not how it works. The consequence was a result of a choice or decision that you made. You can keep lying to yourself by saying, "I don't know how I keep finding myself in these situations," or simply stop underestimating the importance of making good choices and decisions.

When God made man, He made him different than any other creature on earth. He did that by giving us free will, the ability to choose. Of course, that does not mean we get to choose how, when, where, and into what environment we are born, but we are free to choose how we respond to those circumstances. Unfortunately, the downside of free will is that we will and often do make bad decisions. Some of these bad decisions can lead to relatively small inconveniences; however, some can affect or cost us our lives. Again, I say the time to start thinking about and putting this equation into action is now, not later, regardless of your age.

It is critical to your well-being that you think before you act. If you fail to, you will find yourself saying, as some do, "I got caught up." That term is funny in a sad and pathetic kind of way. When I have used that phrase, it sounded like I magically appeared in the consequence portion of the equation. While I can't speak for all, I certainly can speak for myself. When I decided to be honest with myself, I had to admit that the term is nothing more than a weak excuse. In fact, since I am pretty good at knowing and recognizing excuses, I will tell you that "I got caught up" can be interpreted to simply mean, "I made a poor choice, which led to an even worse decision, and that is how I ended up in this situation."

"Discretion will guard you, understanding will watch over you."
—*Proverbs. 2:11*

As humans, we are often guided by emotions, which we will talk about later. And as males, we are often driven by two very powerful emotions—pleasure and anger. Both of these emotions, if not recognized and controlled, can make us extremely shortsighted. This lack of clear vision and an incomplete thought process can make us speed through the choices and decision portion of the equation, and we quickly find ourselves in negative consequences. By then it's usually too late, as the act has already been completed and cannot be undone. You don't have to be a genius to see and understand that, no matter the situation, it is to your benefit to slow things down and take the time to think before you act and find yourself in a negative consequence.

When I was growing up, my mom used a coffee cup to illustrate a visual teaching tool for me to use when analyzing situations—and no, she did not have to throw it at me this time. She held the coffee cup in her hand and turned it completely around and upside down. She said that before I made a choice that would lead to an important decision, I needed to make sure I looked at the situation from all angles, all sides, the top, and the bottom like she was demonstrating with the cup. When she first told me this, I admit that I didn't totally get it, but I never forgot it. Later I realized she was telling me that no matter the situation, I needed to ensure that I took the time to consider it from all angles before making the decision to act.

More times than not, when I use this little tool things work a lot better for me than when I choose not to think before I act. I can honestly say that my biggest mistakes in life came when I failed to "look at the whole cup." When you use this tool, it is extremely important that you be completely honest with yourself. Failure to be honest will give you false results because you will come up with the conclusion you want instead of the best outcome. You will only see the good and totally ignore the negatives by not turning the cup all the way around and upside down. By not being honest, you only punish yourself. Remember, you can lie to everyone if you choose to, but you can't lie to yourself. You may start to believe your lie, but that doesn't change anything—it's still a lie.

Another way to look at this equation is to think, "If I do *this* (choice and decision), then *that* can happen (consequence.)" If you are not comfortable with the *that*, then don't do the *this*. While our poor choices and decisions can and often do hurt others, it is you who will be held accountable and responsible for the results of your actions. *Accountable* is defined in part as "obliged to account for one's acts (explainable)." *Responsible* is defined as "able to distinguish between right and wrong, and to think and act rationally."

As you can see, the words *consequence, accountability,* and *responsibility* are closely related. Please don't ever forget that it is you who will ultimately suffer the consequences of your actions. It is you who will be held accountable and responsible for your poor choices and decisions. Often when we make poor choices and decisions, we either make excuses for our actions or point our finger and blame someone else for them. Both are weak attempts to deflect our actions onto someone else instead of accepting responsibility for them. Being a man includes holding yourself accountable and responsible for your actions. That does not give you a right to not make good, sound choices and decisions, but hopefully, it will make you think before you act.

Since you are responsible for your actions, you need to be extremely careful about from whom you take advice before making your decisions. Ask yourself if the person you are taking advice from truly has your best interests in mind. Also, ask yourself if the person from whom you are seeking advice has experienced positive consequences of their own choices and decisions. If the person does not make good decisions in his or her own life, how can he or she give you advice on yours? Now, if the person from whom you are seeking advice acknowledges those poor decisions and gives you advice that has come from experience, you may want to consider what he or she has to say. There is absolutely nothing wrong with seeking information to help you come to a positive conclusion; just don't forget that you are still responsible for the outcome of your decisions. If the reason you did something was because so-and-so told you to do it, that is just another excuse and will not be acceptable. Be responsible and consider getting good information to help you come to a positive conclusion. Ensure that you don't use the advice of others as an easy way out, letting someone else make your decisions for you in matters of doing the right thing.

Often, things can happen that will require you to work through the equation fast. There are times when the consequence is staring you in the face and you will say it happened quickly, but in reality you did have time to analyze your choices and decisions but failed to do so, thus making the consequence appear to have happened suddenly. For example, let's say that your boys come to pick you up to go to a party that you know is in a bad area. You know that you have no business going to the party, and you also know that there will be drugs and alcohol there. You minimize the situation by telling yourself, "It's just a party," and you *choose* to disregard all the contributing factors, which leads to your *deciding* to go to the party. Don't act surprised when you and your boys experience *negative consequences* by being in the wrong place at the wrong time. So when the police ask you what happened, please don't say, "I don't know. Things happened so quickly, and I just got caught up." No, you had a choice not to go to the party, but you decided to go anyway, despite all the indicators that told you it was not a good idea. Part of making good choices and decisions is avoiding unnecessary and risky behavior. You can minimize all you want, which is up to you. It is your choice, and it is you who will suffer the consequences of your bad choices and decisions. I am not telling you what to do; I am telling you that you need to think about these things as you make this journey.

With all that said, you can still think before you act, and it may still lead to a bad decision. We are all human and all make mistakes, but we are still held accountable for our actions. I will tell you that your chances for positive outcomes are much better when you take the time to stop and think before you act. Hopefully, you minimize your life-altering decisions and learn from these mistakes. The way to show you have learned from a poor decision is not to repeat it. Mistakes are often difficult life lessons, so at least make them into positive life lessons by not repeating them. Remember, constantly repeated poor decisions are no longer mistakes; they are now habits. And negative habits cannot possibly lead to positive results in the end. Another way to say it is, "Poor choices and decisions do not lead to positive consequences."

Now the opposite is also true: well-meaning positive consequences come from making good choices and decisions. Start making a habit of making good decisions. As I mentioned earlier, the time to start that habit is now. Like anything worth having in life, making good habits, including making good decisions, takes dedicated thought, hard work, and lots of practice by the training of the mind. Please don't wait until the big things are upon you before you decide to start utilizing the equation. Start with small things in everyday life so that you start to train your mind to think before you act. It's not hard, but it will require taking responsibility for your actions and practicing good decision making.

A personal example is when I chose and then decided not to go to class. The consequence or result was that I received five F's on my report card, which further led to my mother snatching my car. I concluded that I didn't like the consequences of my decisions. I had absolutely no one to blame; it was up to me to start making better choices. This situation forced me to be accountable and responsible for my actions. I decided I wanted to graduate, so I had to come up with a plan of action and put it into motion. Then and only then did the results turn toward the positive. Remember, you have to use the whole equation. I did want to graduate, but I had to decide to come up with a plan and put it into motion. Then things could move in the right direction, toward positive results. Had I only chosen to graduate without deciding to put the plan into action, the choice by itself would not have meant anything. Even a positive choice without a decision to act is useless. In fact, a choice without the action can lead to another one of those empty excuses like, "I was going to but..." No, it's not always going to be easy making good decisions, but since your very life can hang in the balance, it is worth any and all of your efforts. Besides, I never said anything about this being easy, so just know that going forward.

The reality of it is that some of you will truly take the equation to heart, but unfortunately some of you will choose to do it your way. Hopefully it won't be too late when you finally realize your way just isn't working. Since this is about choices, it is up to you to decide which category you will choose: the one that takes the equation to heart, or the one that chooses to ignore it and take the hard road by doing it his own way.

> *"For the Lord gives wisdom; from His mouth come knowledge and understanding."*
> —*Proverbs 2:6*

There are a few other crucial words associated with the equation to help you in your decision-making process. The first is knowledge—"the fact or state of knowing; the perception of fact or truth; clear and certain mental apprehension." The more positive information you can store in your mental database, the more you have with which to make better choices and decisions to help avoid negative consequences. We will talk more on this subject later, but for now just know that you can never have too much knowledge. Also, never forget that knowledge not utilized serves no purpose. This means that you can know everything there is to know, or think you do, but if you don't put it to work, it is useless. Not all knowledge is positive. An example would be if you only put things into your brain that are negative, it cannot lead to making positive choices and decisions. Let's say you know a lot about selling drugs and committing crimes. How is that knowledge going to translate into making positive, life-enhancing decisions? Positive results simply do not come from negativity, and that includes negative data stored in your brain.

Another word we need to discuss is *judgment*, which is defined as "the ability to judge, make a decision, or form an opinion objectively, authoritatively, and wisely, especially in matters affecting action; good sense; discretion." Again, you can see these words are very closely related. Although the equation is based on a simple formula, there is more to it than initially meets the eye. To make the best choices that will point you in the right direction, you need good judgment. Good judgment will help you recognize the difference between a positive choice and a negative one. Positive knowledge drives good judgment.

The final piece to bring this all together is *wisdom*, simply the act of being wise. To act means to do something, so *wisdom* is our action word. If knowledge and good judgment help you make good choices and decisions, then wisdom is where you put the knowledge and judgment to work for a positive outcome. Wisdom is invisible, so it must show itself through wise actions. The journey to manhood is about making good choices and decisions, not having good intentions without taking wise actions. Embrace the equation as if your life depended on it—because it does. Knowing the equation without putting it into action daily serves no purpose. I once read that life is about the choices you make and not the chances you take.

> *"Take my instruction and not silver, and knowledge rather than choicest gold. For wisdom is better than jewels; and all desirable things cannot compare with her."*
> —*Proverbs 8:10–11*

CHAPTER 3
IDENTITY

In the previous chapter, we talked extensively about the importance of making good choices that lead to good decisions and positive consequences. Not only will you see it often in one form or another throughout this book, but more importantly you will need it on your life journey.

Moving forward, let's talk about identity. When I say *identity*, I'm talking about your personal identity—not only who you are now, but more importantly who you wish to become in the future. You may not have a choice of the parents you are born to or the environment in which you presently find yourself. However, you certainly have some say in the type of man you desire to become as you progress in life.

Numerous traits go into the making of a man. We are going to be talking about a few that I believe are necessary to define your identity. This section is about giving you some tools to consider as you proceed. The information I am sharing is not intended to make you popular, but if you are successful in establishing these traits, it will definitely make you stand out. There will be something different about you. What will be different is your character, which will stand out amongst the crowd. Being a man is not about being popular. It's about doing the right thing simply because it's the right thing to do. It's about doing the right thing even when no one is looking. Let's establish this right now regarding doing the right thing—if you are only doing the right thing because it may be popular or because you are being watched, then you are building your identity on shallow ground. Your motivation should not be either of those reasons, but it should simply be because it is the right thing to do.

The personality traits of a man should be those that have deep roots and therefore can withstand adversity. These are traits that hold fast when it's not popular and even when it feels like you are standing alone. It has been said, "A man who stands for nothing will fall for anything." Being a man of true character can often be difficult and lonely. It is not easy to go against the crowd even if the crowd is collectively wrong. A man will stand his ground even if it means he has to do it alone and go against the crowd. Going along with the crowd because you don't want to appear "weak or scary" is another sad excuse. It's an odd excuse because if you go along with the crowd even if you know it is not the right thing to do, you are acting weak because you are letting others dictate your actions. And you are acting scary because you choose to go along with the crowd instead of standing up for the right thing. Being a man means you stand out because of your character, not because you follow others in doing the wrong thing.

> *"And the rain fell, and the floods came, and the winds blew and slammed against that house; and yet it did not fall, for it had been founded on the rock."*
> —*Matthew 7:25*

Just as a home builder doesn't build a house without putting serious thought into what goes into the foundation of the house, you also should put serious thought into what goes into the foundation of your identity. It doesn't make any difference how big, how pretty, or how much the house cost; if it is not built on a solid foundation, then when the storm comes it is going to crumble and fall. Only a foolish person would build his house directly on the sand. To be the man I hope you become, it is important that you first build a solid foundation (character) so that when trouble comes, your house (identity) is not demolished.

In this chapter, we will talk about several materials (traits) you will need to consider to build your foundation. Where you are in your journey (younger or older) will determine whether you need to build your foundation from scratch, do some preventive maintenance, or even do a complete reconstruction of your present foundation. An absolute must as we begin is that you will need to do an in-depth inspection of your present foundation. Doing this requires 100 percent complete honesty with yourself. Remember, you can lie to others but not to yourself. During this inspection, if you see cracks (character flaws) in your foundation, don't ignore them. Acknowledge them and get to work immediately on repairing them. If you don't like something about your character, change it. As with any cracks found in the foundation, if they are left unattended, they will eventually lead to additional problems and sometimes complete, unrepairable damage.

Do not forget that since we are human, we are flawed and by no means perfect. On our journey, perfection is a destination that we must continually seek, knowing very well, however, that we will never arrive. This simply means that you will never be perfect, but that must never deter you from always seeking to better yourself by recognizing and, most importantly, doing something about those imperfections and flaws (cracks in your foundation). The easy thing to say is, "Oh, that's just the way I am." Sorry to tell you, fellas, but while there may be some truth to that statement, as we are all born with certain personality traits, that is still a cop-out. And it does not excuse you of your responsibility for doing the right thing. It's not easy to admit fault in yourself, but that is what a man must do. You must first admit there is a problem in need of repair before you can fix it. There is nothing wrong with acknowledging that you have faults; the problems come when you know of your flaws but choose to do nothing about them.

A man must be honest with himself to identify not only his strengths but his weaknesses as well. So let's get started on some of the specific traits I believe you will need on your journey.

Character

This is what truly defines what kind of man you are or desire to become. It is important that you start to determine your character now as it is something that requires a lifetime to develop. Character development is a slow process. You have to decide to start living your life in a manner that supports the man you wish to be. *Character* is defined as "features and traits that form the individual nature of a person, reputation, and qualities." Your words may tell the world what you wish to be known as, but it is your character that shows the world the real you. Your actions speak much louder than anything you can ever say. Your mouth may proclaim you to be one way, but your character is the bright light that reveals the true you. Your words may initially get you some attention, but it is your actions (character) that make people sit up and want to see what kind of man you really are. Unfortunately, many males talk a good game, but fewer stand up to the real test of their character.

Personally, I don't think we as males give our character enough thought. Your character tells the world who you are and what you stand for. Something that makes such a profound statement is worthy of serious thought. Should you fail to give your character serious thought, your actions will show that you couldn't care less how the world perceives you. Either way, you will still be telling the world who you are by your actions. Here is an example of your actions defining your character: Let's say you are a person who continually finds himself in negative consequences as a result of constant poor choices and bad decisions. After a while, you will just be seen as a person who always makes bad decisions, and the world will just assume that is who you are. You may even start to believe that about yourself. You may start to take the attitude, "If that's what they think about me, then that's who I'm going to be." That kind of attitude does nothing but hurt you. Instead, put some serious thought into what kind of man you want to be known as and start building your foundation to support your desire. You can also choose to be a person who constantly demonstrates positive character traits, and that is what people will see in you. Either way, it is important that you take the time now to do a self-analysis of who you are and determine whether that is who you wish to be. If you fail to work on your character identity, please believe me when I say that society will gladly give you one, and more often than not they will be wrong. It is even more important for us as men of color since society may already have an ill-conceived notion of who we are, so we must self-define our character before it is done for us.

There is still a large number of white Americans who believe us to be lazy, good-for-nothing individuals who are prone to acts of criminality and lacking the ability to control our actions. We know that this is entirely too broad a stroke with which to paint us as a people. We know this is extremely unfair and a biased thought process. Understand that this type of thinking is based on ignorance. Ignorance is not always stupidity; it is simply an act of not knowing. That is exactly why you need to define the character you wish to be known for instead of letting society do it for you. It is important that you represent yourself well by being a man of good character. To reflect true positive character to others, it is important that you know who you are first. This is where it is important that you be brutally honest with yourself. You can only fake positive character for so long. Sooner or later, your real character will reveal itself, and you will be exposed. Failure to be 100 percent honest with yourself during your self-inspection only hurts you in the long run.

You need to know that change, particularly in your character, does not come easy, nor does it come fast. That is why this I call this a journey and not just a destination book. You will never move in the right direction on this journey if you refuse to acknowledge your shortcomings. You could always go with the way of thinking that there is nothing wrong with you and that it is everyone else who has a problem. If that sounds like another excuse, you are very correct. It is an excuse used by those who deny the truth about themselves and aren't willing to put in the hard work to better themselves. As Helen Keller said, "Character cannot be developed in ease and quiet. Only through experience of trial and suffering can the soul be strengthened, ambition inspired, and success achieved."

I recall many occasions in my life when I had to take a hard look at myself and admit there were flaws in my character that I didn't like. One of those occasions is the incident I mentioned earlier when my mom attacked me in my sleep after I had told her to see if she could get another ride when she was stranded. That had a lot to do with my losing my precious car. While getting beat up and losing my car did hurt, what hurt the most was the fact that my character was so lacking that I was the kind of person who wouldn't even pick up his mother when she needed help. I was supposed to be the one man in all the world that she could finally count on, but I failed her miserably. In my mind, I didn't think I was that bad; however, my actions, or on this occasion my inaction, said an awful lot about my character, and I didn't like it. Remember, actions speak louder than words, and my actions were telling my mom that I was unreliable, thoughtless, and ungrateful. During that same period, my character was showing my boss that I was not responsible or dependable. It also showed my teachers that I didn't have enough sense to even care about my own education.

Speaking of education, let me tell you a quick side story regarding that infamous five F's and one D report card. What I didn't tell you is that the class in which I got the D was gym class. I think the only reason

I got a D and not an F is because I did at least show up some of the time. During this particular semester, the exercise was swimming. Now, if I was entirely too cool to wear the Navy ROTC uniform, there was no way I was going to jump in a pool and watch my hot-combed pressed hair go from hanging down my neck to being seriously "napped up" on the top of my head in a matter of seconds. My gym teacher just also happened to be the head coach of the varsity football team and had been for decades. This man had the voice and appearance you pictured in your mind when you thought of a high school football head coach. One day he caught me after class, he looked me right in the eye, and said, "Son, there is way more to life than just being cool." For some reason, that simple statement shook me to my core, and I have never forgotten it. Again, my actions were making a profound statement about my character, and I was not proud of it at all.

After the light had started to shine brightly on my shallow character, I didn't go to my mother, boss, or teachers and say, "Hey, I realize I have some serious character flaws, and I want you to know I am going to change my ways." I think I already understood that the people in my world didn't care to hear what I had to say; they wanted to see my actions. That's when I began working on myself to show people that I was responsible and dependable and that I did care about my education.

A couple of quick points before we move on. While you may admire certain character traits in others, don't try to be exactly like anyone else. God made only one you. We may have similarities, but you are one of a kind. Find and embrace your positive uniqueness. You can take some positive characteristics you admire in others and add them to your uniqueness. Also, along that same line, please don't pick up and copy the negative character traits of others. We will talk more on this later, but if you hang out with those of negative character, people will not bother to find out who you are. They will automatically associate you with the others. Just like when I dressed like and hung out with the thuggish crowd, people naturally assumed I was a thug, which wasn't really who I was. You will learn, if you don't already know, that society will judge you quickly—sometimes by your actions, your words, or merely by your appearance. This is just something to think about: if you want your true identity to be shown, it will be up to you to shine the best light on how you wish to be seen. *Life Lesson*: As a whole, the world (society) doesn't love you and doesn't have time to get to know you. So it is up to you to show the best of yourself from the start. However, to show your positive character, you first need to have one.

> *"Do not be deceived: Bad company corrupts good morals."*
> —*1 Corinthians 15:33*

Conscience

Your conscience is that inner sense of what is right and wrong. Conscience is the character trait that will guide you to do the right thing when no one is looking. It's that inner voice that tells you not to do something and that convicts you (makes you feel bad) when you do something you shouldn't have; you chose to minimize that voice and did it anyway. That same inner voice is the one you need to learn to listen to because it can keep you out of trouble or give you peace of mind, knowing you did the right thing. This inner voice can sometimes scream in your head or give you that tight, knot feeling in the pit of your stomach. However, most often it will come in the form of a slight whisper, and if you aren't paying attention, you will miss it altogether. Personally, I don't think it is missed as much as it is just ignored. You know that inner discussion you have with yourself before and after you got busted doing something that you shouldn't have been? You know, the one that says, "I knew I shouldn't have done that"? That was your conscience talking to you, but you chose to ignore it.

In my case, when I made a poor decision and chose a negative consequence, I simply ignored my conscience when it was trying to warn me of a bad situation. We will often choose to ignore the inner voice because it appears to be easier and more fun to do wrong over right. I use the word *appears* because the result is usually a negative consequence and there is nothing fun about that. Another point to remember when making choices and decisions is that everything that feels right or fun isn't necessarily so. So if your conscience is nagging you about something, that is your clue that you should take some additional time to analyze your present situation. Christians call this inner voice the Holy Spirit, which is given to believers when they accept Jesus as their Savior. Regardless of your religious beliefs, I believe we are all born with a sense of knowing the difference between right and wrong. Don't forget that knowing the difference and doing the right thing are not the same.

> *"In that they show that the work of the Law written in their hearts, their consciences also bearing witness and their thoughts alternately accusing or else defending them."*
> —*Romans 2:15*

Discipline

Discipline is "an activity, exercise, or regimen that develops or improves a skill; behavior in accord with rules of conduct." You will need this characteristic to put some of the other upcoming traits to work. Discipline is an "action" or "doing" trait that you will need to tell yourself no or keep yourself from doing something you know is wrong. This is also the trait you will need to make yourself do something you know is right but not necessarily fun or popular. I mentioned earlier that knowing the right thing to do and doing the right thing are different, and discipline is what you will need to do the right thing. Discipline is the hard work I've been talking about. It doesn't come automatically; it needs to be nurtured, developed, and practiced daily. This is the trait that pushes you to develop those positive habits we talked about earlier. To be successful in life, it is mandatory that you continually train this trait as you travel on your journey.

There is nothing easy about developing discipline, but by now you know that this book is not about things being easy. Just as we are all different, this trait and others may be easier for some and more difficult for others. If you find yourself in the latter group, all it means is that you have to work harder. Just because something does not come easily to you, it does not give you an excuse to not pursue it. Regarding the character trait of discipline, even the ones who make it look easy had to work hard at it until it became a positive habit.

You see the need for and the results of discipline all around you every day. When you see a high-level athlete, you can guarantee it took extreme discipline to get to that point of expertise. Yes, some of them were born with God-given ability. However, it is the discipline that makes them train daily to fine-tune that ability when they would rather do something else. Instead, they put their bodies through the pain and suffering of intense training. It takes discipline to get up every day to go to a job that you may or may not like. It is that same discipline that is required to do something that you may not want to do but know it needs to be done.

Discipline can be self-instilled based on expectations you have of yourself, or it can be forced on you in an informal or formal setting. Informally, it can be expected from you by your parents, guardians, or school. Formally, it can be demanded from you in society in the form of obeying rules and laws. Either way, you get to choose whether or not to conform to those expectations. Failure to conform to parents, guardians, or school can get you punished or kicked out of school. Failure to conform to the rules and laws of society can lead you to getting locked up in prison. There is also the form of discipline that is thrust upon you in basic training in the military. You learn very quickly that there are rules in the military and that there are negative consequences if those are broken. The navy was an intense introduction to discipline for me, but it did point me in the right direction of being a man. I still consider it one of my best early moves in my journey.

What we tend to miss on the subject of discipline is that it is required in all aspects of life. Let's say you aspire to be a professional athlete or an attorney. You may have the dream, but it means nothing if you don't have the self-discipline to do the work it takes to attain that goal. You see, I used the term *self-discipline* because it is one thing to respond when someone is pushing you but quite another when it's just you. Just like doing the right thing even when no one is looking, it takes discipline to do the right thing regardless of who may or may not be watching. Discipline should not be something you can just pick and choose to direct certain parts of your life. You can have the discipline to train to be the professional athlete you desire to be. However, you need to be just as disciplined in your education and other everyday responsibilities. Let's say you are disciplined enough in your training to be a professional athlete but lack the same discipline to stay away from the people you know you shouldn't be around, to properly manage your finances, or to make good choices and decisions. Even as a highly trained athlete, without discipline you may find yourself still stuck in negative consequences with a strong possibility of all of your years of training being for nothing in the end. If you don't believe me, just pay attention to the news filled with stories of professional athletes who failed to use the same discipline it took them to get into their sport in the other areas of their life. These men and women are finding themselves broke after having made millions of dollars. Some are finding themselves in prison or worse. The one thing they all had in common is that they knew what discipline looked like but failed to utilize it in all aspects of their lives.

Discipline takes daily focus and practice. Discipline can be trained by focusing on the things you know you should do and avoiding the things you shouldn't. It can be from something as simple as not eating or drinking something that's not healthy for you to more challenging actions such as not hanging around people who are a hindrance and contrary to your attaining your goals.

> *"He will die for lack of instruction, and in the greatness of his folly he will go astray."*
>
> *—Proverbs 5:23*

Ethics and Morals

These character traits we have discussed and the ones to follow go hand in hand. Ethics can be explained as a system of principles or rules of conduct. Morals are the senses within you that cause you to conform to the rules of right conduct, and ethics are the rules that govern us as a society. While some ethics may vary based on cultural differences, there are what I will call general ethics that are, for the most part, universal. Of course, there are exceptions to the rule. I would say a general ethical principle is that you should not take the life of another. I am sure in certain cultures there are exceptions, but for the sake of argument, let's say as a general universal rule you shouldn't take the life of another. Now we all know that this rule is broken on a daily basis in our communities, cities, country, and across the entire planet. Can you imagine how much worse it would be in society if there were no ethical principles? Things are bad now, but without ethics to govern us, it would be so much worse. For a society to function properly, it is important that we have ethical principles and morally correct people who conform to or abide by those principles. That is why I included these particular character traits in the makeup of a man of high character.

Ethics are the rules of conduct, or how you should govern yourself, and morals are the actual adherence to those established ethics. This principle is displayed when you know what is ethical and demonstrate that knowledge by carrying yourself in a morally correct manner. Again, knowing the rules (ethics) means nothing if you do not abide (moralistic behavior) by those ethics. Support and demonstrate your knowledge with your actions.

As I write this book, Americans are gearing up to elect the next president of the United States. When the political races first started, many in the running claimed to be fine, upstanding, ethical citizens. However, as time went on, secrets started to come out that called their morals into question. As it turned out, their ethical-sounding words were not supported by their nonmoralistic behavior. Actions always speak louder than words. "Character is like a tree and reputation is like a shadow," Abraham Lincoln said. "The shadow is what we think of it, and the tree is the real thing."

Strive to be a man of high ethical character strongly supported by moral behavior. Ethics and morals are nothing more than knowing the right thing to do and doing it. These are not traits that you can just talk about. Your actions and how you carry yourself will tell the world you are an ethical and a morally sound person.

> *"Boast no more so very proudly, do not let arrogance come from your mouth; For the LORD is a God of knowledge and by Him, actions are weighed."*
> —*1 Samuel 2:3*

Values

Values is a word often associated with ethics and morals. However, ethics are usually accepted rules that govern a society. Values can differ from person to person or group to group as they show what a person or group deems important. They can be positive or negative. Individual or group values do not outweigh societal ethics. For example, the values of a law enforcement entity are generally considered positive. Law enforcement values greatly differ from those of a criminal enterprise, which are usually deemed negative. A man of high character should encompass values that at least parallel to those of society. However, personally, I believe your values should even be higher than those established by society. Just because society may deem something acceptable or not illegal does not necessarily make it right. As a man of high character, you need to set the bar high for yourself and not lower it to compromise what you believe. As an example, something that is deemed legal or acceptable in society may go against a Christian's values because it may be contrary to the Word of God.

Integrity

Another word associated with ethics, morals, and values is *integrity*, which is the strict adherence to ethical and moral principles. To be considered a man of integrity is very high praise indeed. It means you stand firm in your moral behavior. One who has integrity is extremely sound not only in word but more importantly in deed (action). A man of true integrity can be depended upon to do the right thing. I believe integrity is the culmination of ethics and morals that are foundationally sound. Dr. Martin Luther King Jr. had this to say about integrity: "When your character is built on a spiritual and moral foundation, your contagious way of life will influence millions."

> *"He who walks in integrity walks securely, but he who perverts his ways will be found out."*
> —*Proverbs 10:9*

Honesty

Another mandatory trait of a high-character man is honesty (being honest, upright, freedom from deceit or fraud). If a man lacks the ability to be truthful, then his words and actions will be clouded by doubt from others. Just as your actions need to support your words, your words should mirror your actions. Seek to be a man of your word. If you say you are going to do something, ensure that you do it. If for some reason you are unable to do what you said, make sure you let the person know in advance. However, this should be the exception and not the rule. A man of high character stands by his word. Once you are deemed a liar or someone who is not honest, nothing that comes out of your mouth after that is given any real merit. Honesty and truthfulness are mandatory for a man of real honorable character.

> *"Righteous lips are the delight of kings, and he one who speaks right is loved."*
>
> —*Proverbs 16:13*

Fortitude, Resilience, Courage

Next, we have a group of traits that you should desire as you build the foundation of your character: fortitude, resilience, and courage. Fortitude is "the mental and emotional strength in facing adversity." Fortitude is what it takes to be and stay mentally strong when the hard times kick in. Resilience is closely related to fortitude. It is what allows you to endure the hard times with fortitude. It enables you to bounce back and not quit after the adversity comes.

I have mentioned several times that life is not easy; well, these are the attributes (traits) you will need to get through the difficult times. You can have all the ethics, morals, values, honesty, and integrity in the world and still endure trying times. In fact, tough times are a guarantee in life; we all have them. What a man must do is recognize them for what they are, and that is a challenge for your character to truly reveal what type of man you are. You can submit to these challenges and let them beat you down, or you can accept them with fortitude and resilience. These trying times will challenge you and can make you want to throw your hands up and quit. There is a saying that goes, "Tough times don't last, but tough people do." Fortitude and resilience are the traits that give you the strength to hang in there no matter what. My most revealing character growth spurts have come during times of adversity. These are the times you truly learn what you are made of. These are the times you find out that you can handle more than you ever thought. Anybody can portray strength during the quiet and peaceful times, but the real challenge is when the tests of life come at you.

"I can do all things through Him who strengthens me."
—Philippians 4:13

If you prepare your character foundation with the traits we have discussed, it will help you get through those times. You may not recognize it while you are going through the trial, but once you get through and look back, you will have a sense of accomplishment because you faced what life had thrown at you, and you survived. You can survive as long as you don't quit, and fortitude and resilience will help you not quit. The time to prepare for these trying times is not when the storm hits. Build your foundation before it hits; prepare now. You can't just say to yourself when the tough times come, *I know I will have the fortitude and resilience to endure the storm.* It doesn't work like that. That's like saying when I see the storm down the street, "I will work on the foundation of my house." Train yourself in these traits during the smaller trials in life, and then you will have the right mind-set and these traits will grow as you grow. Another example is that a boxer's first fight isn't against the champ. He trains and fights his way up the ranks first, and then he takes on the champ. Sometimes you take on the champ and you lose. It's the same way in life—sometimes you win and sometimes you lose. If you get knocked down, you get back up and fight. If you get knocked out, then when you wake up, get your butt up, go back to training, and get back in the ring. The only time you truly lose is when you refuse to get back in the fight.

Courage

Courage is "the quality of mind or spirit that enables a person to face difficulty, danger, pain, without fear; bravery." It is courage that you will need to stand firm when attacked, be it mentally or physically. It is courage that allows you to stand firm in the face of turmoil and chaos. You will need the courage to stand firm when your morals, values, and integrity come into question. It is courage that allows you to stand firm when your fortitude and resilience are wavering and you want to give in and quit. Remember, courage and bravery are not the absence of fear; they are the traits needed to allow you to stand firm although you may be afraid. Fear is healthy as long as you don't allow it to make you unable to act. Courage is not the absence of fear but the conquering of it.

> *"Be strong and courageous. Do not be afraid or tremble at them, for the Lord your God is the one who goes with you. He will not fail you or forsake you."*
> —*Deuteronomy 31:6*

Pride and Humility

Let's discuss two character traits that some may consider to be opposites. I believe pride and humility are needed to provide balance in a man. I think it is important that a man have a sense of pride in himself. When I talk about pride, I don't mean it in terms of arrogance. I mean it as "pleasure or satisfaction taken in something done by, or belonging to oneself." I believe it to be a sense of self-respect and self-esteem reflected in the way you present and carry yourself. You must first respect yourself and others before you can expect others to respect you. Here's a quick related side note regarding respect: Please don't ever get fear and respect for someone mixed up. They are not the same thing. People can fear you because you threatened them with harm, but that is not the same thing as respect. They may even despise or hate you, but that does not translate to respect. This confusion regarding respect is a major problem among our young men. There are entirely too many men locked up in prison for long periods of time because of what they perceived as disrespect. Respect is earned by being a man of character, not by how much harm you can threaten or inflict upon another person.

Now back to pride and humility. It is one thing to have pride in yourself, but it is another thing altogether when your pride is shown as arrogance and you act as if you are superior to others. There is nothing appealing about a man who has to constantly tell others of his self-perceived greatness. When I see this type of behavior in a man, all I see is a person who is trying to convince himself of his self-worth. It's like building a house on a weak foundation. It will not take much of a storm to blow this house down because its foundation is not solid. Understand that it is not about how much money you make, how nice your stuff may be, or how well you can do something that makes you a man. It is how you carry yourself with the characteristics we have discussed.

The problem with excessive pride is that it makes you think you are better than others or better than you are. This assumption is usually based on something superficial, which can be taken away from you in the blink of an eye. Let's say you base your entire self-worth on being rich, strong, handsome, fast, or any other adjective. Who would you be if you were to lose it all tomorrow? Would you lose your entire identity or self-worth? That is why it is important that you establish your character on a solid foundation built with materials (traits) we have been addressing in this chapter. Granted, the person of high character could also lose everything tomorrow as well. However, because his identity is based on character and not something fleeting, he will still stand firm to endure the adversity with fortitude and resilience.

> *"But let him who boasts, boast of this, that he understands and knows Me, that I am the LORD who exercises lovingkindness, justice and righteousness on earth for I delight in these things, declares the LORD."*
>
> —*Jeremiah 9:24*

This is where humility comes into play. Humility or being humble is the state of not thinking of oneself greater than he should. Being a humble man does not mean you are without pride in yourself or respect, nor without confidence. A humble man does not find it necessary to tell the world of his greatness. A humble man will let his actions and his character speak for him. A humble man is greatly appreciative of his blessings. He does not feel the need to be arrogant regarding his God-given talents, gifts, or abilities. A prideful man will say, "Look how smart, how rich, how successful I have made myself," but a humble man knows that although he too may be smart, rich, or successful, it is not because of his greatness but God's blessings upon him.

Think about this: how can you brag or be arrogant about how smart you are if you did not create your brain? You may have put information in it, but you did not create it. The same can be said regarding your physical appearance and abilities. You may have worked on what God has given you, but it is foolish to think you are the creator of you. If you are the creator of yourself, then stop yourself from getting older and dying one day. A humble man understands his limitations and is much more grateful for his gifts. In my experience, it is the humble man who is more apt to utilize his God-given talents, gifts, and abilities for the betterment of others. The prideful man who believes he created himself is more apt to think selfishly and only use his gifts to further his own selfish agenda. After all, since they created themselves, they believe everyone should create themselves as well. I am a strong believer that the talents, gifts, and abilities given to you are not for you alone but for those you encounter along your journey. You should build others up and share what God has given you. I have also learned that it is best that you learn to humble yourself before life (God) does it for you.

> "When pride comes, then comes disgrace, but with humility comes wisdom."
>
> —Proverbs 11:2

So far in this chapter, I have talked a lot about some positive character traits that I believe will help create the identity of a man—not just an adult male, but a real man whose identity is based on a solid, high-character foundation. Never forget that just because you were born with a penis, it does not automatically make you a man. Whether or not you will evolve into manhood is unknown; however, you do have major input into your outcome.

These are just a few of the primary traits that I feel are vital in setting the foundation for what it takes to be a man. These are the ones I seek to base my identity on. I say *seek* because it is a continued journey more than a destination. During my journey, I have learned that to be successful in anything worth doing, it is important that you have the correct mind-set and focus on the goal at hand. *Mind-set* to me means that you establish a purpose and goal and you focus intently on attaining that goal. It means that anything that interferes with the attainment of that goal is a distraction, and distractions cannot be allowed.

It is important that you focus your mind-set on objectives that result in positive outcomes and not those that lead to negative consequences. Regarding our present topic of identity, I have chosen to focus my mind-set on the traits we have been discussing. The contrary can also be true as well. Let's say that instead of building positive character traits, I focused my mind-set on being the very best drug dealer. It's possible I could attain that goal; however, the negative consequences associated with that mind-set do not correspond to the type of character I desire to possess. It is extremely important that you build your foundation with materials of a positive nature if you desire to be a man of high character.

One of the primary purposes that I wrote this book is to share some of my experiences, even the negative ones. Hopefully, some of you will learn from my mistakes and not do the same. The traits we have been discussing are lofty trait goals, but they are by no means unattainable. However, it will require a focused mind-set and determination. You must understand that on this journey you will make mistakes; it is just a given in life. When you do make a mistake, you must acknowledge it and use it as a lesson on what not to do in the future. Do not—I repeat, do not—use mistakes as an excuse to stay down and not get back in the fight. You live, you make mistakes, and you learn. It is my hope that some things from this book will help you to minimize the seriousness of those mistakes. Whatever you do, you cannot give up on yourself and quit.

I have a granddaughter who is a bit of a perfectionist and extremely competitive. When she was younger and we played a game that she felt she wasn't particularly good at, she would say in frustration, "I'm not good at this. You guys just play without me." That is the easy way out, to quit when things get hard. Of course I didn't let her quit; I just made it a teaching moment. Attaining these traits can be extremely challenging, and on occasion you will fail. Don't you give up and quit! Most of society expects you to take the easy road and quit when things get bumpy. Don't give them that.

Many times on my journey, I have failed miserably at exhibiting some of these traits. Afterward, I felt sorry for myself and wanted to tell the world that I wasn't good at this man thing and they should just move on without me. I eventually picked myself up, took a hard look at myself, analyzed my failure, and then came up with another plan of action. I may have failed numerous times, but what I didn't do was quit. I also didn't stop believing that somewhere deep inside me, I could and would be the type of man I desired to be.

Never stop believing in yourself! Even when you have repeatedly been told you are nothing and will never amount to anything, don't you dare believe that nonsense. Prove them wrong by your actions. Like I said, it won't be easy. You will need determination to build your identity foundation with characteristics mentioned in this chapter.

> *"When I was a child, I used to speak like a child, reason like a child; when I became a man, I did away with childish things."*
>
> *—1 Corinthians 13:11*

4

EMOTIONS

So far we have talked about some pretty serious subjects—no need to stop now. Next up is emotions, which is not exactly the favorite subject of most men. I think men tend to have an unrealistic, preconceived notion of how a man is supposed to feel and act in certain situations. If you watch television, movies, or listen to today's rap music, you probably have come to the conclusion that men are emotionless beings and that any sign of having feelings is an indicator of weakness. This mentality is inaccurate and may confuse some people because, inside, you may feel one way but you may think society expects you to act and feel another way or not feel at all. These mixed messages can cause internal conflict. It has been my experience that the more I know about something, the better I can recognize it when it comes my way. It helps me to make better decisions and hopefully minimize negative consequences. In this chapter, we will discuss emotions and other related areas not so much to make you an expert on the subject but more for you to be aware of them and how they can affect your thought process.

As males, we are prone to put up emotion-deflecting walls to shield ourselves from others. When dealing with other males, we are so concerned with not being viewed as soft or weak that we often go to the extremes to counter that perception. For example, when you are hanging with your friends and another group of males makes even the slightest statement or gives you "a look" you deem threatening or unfriendly, you and your group will probably overreact. Chances are you may feel like if you don't do or say something, you will be viewed as a punk in front of your friends. While this is a form of peer pressure, we are talking about the emotions that feed this type of behavior, which has landed many young men in prison never to feel freedom again.

Now consider that same scenario except this time you are by yourself. Chances are you will likely ignore the other group and just go on your way without issue. What we took away was the feeling that you had to do or say something because of the presence of your friends. It is important that you know and understand the dynamics and related emotions of both situations. The first situation included your and your friends' personal feelings combined with the presence of your boys. You can act in a manner you think is expected of you without giving any real thought to the consequences it could bring to all involved. In the second scenario, in which you are by yourself, your emotions are less likely to flare up because of the absence of your friends, which means there is no additional pressure. Also in the second situation, you are more likely to think clearly because the self-induced "how my friends expect me to feel and act" is not present, so your thought process is less clouded. As a result, you are less likely to get yourself into a negative situation. In the first situation, you chose to respond to what you thought was a form of disrespect, regardless of how minor it may have been. You then decided to act on that choice despite the high probability that it would lead to a negative consequence. It is reasoning like this that it is important for you to learn to control your emotions and feelings; if you don't, they will control you. Unrecognized or uncontrolled emotions can lead to thoughtless choices and decisions. On this journey, anything that you do in a thoughtless manner is going to be followed by negative consequences.

Before you can control your emotions, you must first recognize them and admit that, yes, you are human and are affected by certain feelings. It is also important that we be honest with ourselves and acknowledge our emotions and the things that bother us. If you try and act like nothing bothers you, you are much more prone to negative reactions rather than thinking before you act.

In the last chapter, we talked about creating your identity through positive character traits. If your emotional state is contributing to your acting outside of the character you are creating, then it's time to take a hard look at the problem. Not only do you need to know who you are (character identity), you also need to know what triggers your emotions that can lead to negative actions. By knowing your triggers in advance and the negative actions that could follow, it may help you to avoid those situations altogether. Here's a personal example: I know that I do not like to be in large groups of people when they drink too much and start acting stupid.

So knowing this about myself, I try to minimize my visits to these types of events. I know I can't control how others act, but I can control putting myself in those situations because I know how it frustrates me. Notice I said *minimize* because I am a huge fan of professional football, and I am a card- carrying member of the Raider Nation. So I have to support my team in person at least a couple of times a year. On those days, I know that along with packing my Raider gear, I also need to pack some extra patience.

There are too many emotions and feelings out there to attempt to cover them all. We will cover only a few that I think you will need to be aware of. I want you to know that having feelings does not make you odd, weird, soft, or weak. It makes you human. Take comfort in knowing you are not alone, nor are you the only person to experience these feelings. You must learn to recognize your emotions and the triggers that can activate them, never forgetting to conduct yourself appropriately. I have learned that what truly scares me is the fear of the unknown. If you are aware of your emotions and their triggers when the situations come up, they won't appear as foreign to you.

Early on, I mentioned that most of the subjects that we will discuss in this book are things I wished someone would have talked to me about as a youngster. This chapter on emotions is no different. As I look back on my journey, I can see there were plenty of situations I could have avoided or perhaps made better decisions in had my thoughts not been so clouded or influenced by emotions, which I did not know were so powerful and thought-altering. It wasn't necessarily the emotion that messed me up but the lack of clear thinking that led to poor decisions and negative consequences.

Life lesson: As a man, particularly one of color, there is not one day in your life that you can afford to let your guard down regarding knowing and controlling your actions or reactions due to your emotions. Never forget that you will always be held accountable for your actions regardless of the reason for your emotional state. You may even have a righteous reason for your emotion. However, if that emotion leads to negative behavior, it does not remove your accountability or responsibility. For example, let's say you have a prized, one-of-a-kind possession that absolutely cannot be replaced. As you show it to your best friend, someone who is not paying attention to where he is going bumps into you, causing you to drop the item, which shatters. Not knowing or caring whether he did it on purpose or on accident, your mind goes through a wide range of emotions in a split second. The difference maker is not the emotions but how you deal with the emotions. If you react physically, we know by now that nothing but negative consequences are coming your way. So when the police ask you why you assaulted this person, no reason you give is going to keep you out of jail. Know your emotions and triggers, and control them before they control you.

"Like a city that is broken into and without walls is a man who has no control over his spirit."
                                                                    —Proverbs 25:28

Love

Let's get started with what is probably the most powerful emotion of all, and that is love. This emotion can lead to and include almost every other emotion, good or bad. It can drive men to great heights and even greater lows. By no means am I even close to being an expert in this arena, but I do believe I qualify to share my experiences and observations. On your journey, you will certainly want to be fully aware of what this powerful emotion can do for you and to you, particularly when it goes bad.

Love is one of those words that, if I asked ten people on the street what it means to them, I would get at least eight different responses depending on the age and sex of the person I asked. *Love* is probably one of the most overused words in the English vocabulary. Generally speaking, it is used to define an extreme feeling of personal attachment one has toward another person or even a thing. It is a word that is thrown around entirely too much in today's society. I am just as guilty as everyone else of doing so. People have a love for one another, their family members, pets, vehicles, favorite foods, sports teams—the list goes on and on. However, the most common use of the word *love* is when it is used to describe a romantic feeling one has toward another. Second would probably be the feelings one has toward family and friends. Normally when we talk about love, it makes people think warm, happy thoughts. However, while love can indeed bring joy and happiness, it can bring extremely unpleasant emotions and feelings when a relationship falls apart. Some of these are fear, guilt, loneliness, envy, disappointment, doubt, embarrassment, sorrow, rejection, and the polar opposite of love—hate. It is odd how something that starts off so nice can turn into something so ugly. In some situations, you would be hard pressed to believe that love was ever present. On your journey, you will undoubtedly be affected by the good, the bad, and the ugly of this powerful emotion.

Regarding that long list of feelings I just mentioned that can follow when a relationship has gone bad, I can personally say that I have experienced every one of them plus a few more. I will not lie to you and give you the big, tough guy speech about it being no big thing. It hurts, and it hurts a lot. One of the things that hurt me the most when the love went bad was that everything was so out of control, and regardless of what I tried to do, I could not fix it. I have been on the losing end of love twice in my life. I have had my feelings hurt numerous times, but I have experienced true out-and-out heartbreak only twice, and both times were by the same lady. Talk about being a slow learner, right? The biggest lesson that I eventually learned from those hurts was that I cannot control how another person feels about me, regardless of how I may feel toward her. We are all individuals who have to make our own decisions. Sometimes love starts off and continues as a mutual feeling, and sometimes it doesn't. If a woman does not feel the same way as you do, the bottom line is that no matter how much it hurts, you can't make her love you in return. That is a very hard lesson to learn and accept, but it is a reality, so learn it now and save yourself hardship later.

Along my journey, I have learned that there is a Grand Canyon–size difference between love and lust. Lust is nothing more than the arousal we get when the feelings we have toward a female are solely based on sexual desire. *Life Lesson*: Just because you are physically attracted to a female, it does not automatically mean that you are in love. It could simply mean you are sexually attracted to her. This initial attraction may be a starting point, but by no means is it the final factor in what love is. There is so much more to love and a woman than just physical attraction and sex. Many of us (males and females) have made the mistake of being in relationships solely based on sex, only to find out that outside of sex, we have nothing in common. In fact, you may learn that not only do you not love each other, you may not even really like the other person. I will tell you that sex can bring you together, but sex alone will not keep you together.

For a real relationship to truly evolve into a loving one, it will take much more than sex being the glue that holds it together. Real love takes time to grow. It takes time to really get to know each other—and I mean *really* know each other. That includes the other person's good and bad points. It takes time to understand the other person's likes, dislikes, and the things you have in common (besides sex). One of the problems with premarital sex is that you will tend to base your entire relationship on sex before you have established a solid foundation. There is no doubt in my mind that people are engaging in sexual relationships far too young before they are mentally prepared for that level of intimacy.

Regarding the emotion of love, the main thing I want to get across to you is to be aware in advance of the negative feelings that can follow when what you thought was love turns into something altogether different. More than likely, you are in one of two categories: you have already experienced heartbreak, or you are going to experience it. It doesn't happen to everyone, but it happens to most of us mortals. Some of you have experienced the pain of lost love and have some emotional scars to prove it, but you survived. If you have not experienced it yet, just know that when it comes, it is going to hurt like crazy, but I promise you the world is not going to end. It is one of life's hard lessons, so learn from it and keep moving forward. When it does happen to you, you may need to go back and review the character traits resilience and fortitude, as they will come in handy. Also, know that you are not the first nor will you be the last to have his heart broken. Chalk it up to a life lesson and move on. However, know it will take some time, so be patient.

It's not the heartache that gets you in trouble; it's how you react to it that brings you negative consequences. Love is a very powerful emotion, and if not handled properly it can easily cause you a world of trouble. Here is a perfect personal example of how you can get yourself into trouble behind something that you thought was love but turned out to be something else. Pay close attention because there are many lessons to be learned by my stupidity in this one. Many years ago, in my early journey days, I was nowhere near as experienced in life's hard lessons as I am now.

I was seeing this girl who was nothing but high drama. However, at the time, I was blinded by lust. On this one occasion, she had gotten into it with her ex-boyfriend (and baby daddy). During the disagreement, her ex-boyfriend had slapped her. I was not present for any of this.

Since this dude had slapped the woman I "loved" (lusted for) and I was a man (very loosely stated), I felt I needed to do something about it. So I grabbed my pistol and waited where this guy normally hung out. I waited several hours for him to show up but he never did—and I still thank God for that one. Because had he shown up, this book would have never been written, at least not by me. My story would have been totally different. Hopefully, you are not laughing too hard at me. Like I said, it was extremely stupid, which is exactly why I am writing this book so you don't do something equally as stupid.

I soon found out that the reason they got into it was that she was playing both of us. Here I was about to shoot this dude over some mess I let this girl get me into. I thought I was in love. I also thought that was what a man was supposed to do—defend his girl. I could have ruined my entire life. Had I known about the equation that day, I would have totally flunked that test in a major way. I made a bad choice and decided to act on it by going over there with a gun. I don't need to tell you the negative consequences that would have followed. That is just one of the hard lessons that have caused me to write this book.

Later that same day, after initially thinking about how much of a bad butt I was to go over there, I realized just how stupid of a move it was. I could have shot him or been shot because I do believe I was not the only one with a gun. I could have gone to prison, which is exactly what I had been trying to avoid my whole life. The girl would not have been anywhere to be found. She might have even asked me how I could have shot her baby daddy. I would have tried to blame her for my stupidity, but the reality of it was that I made a bad decision, which definitely would have led me to a terrible consequence.

Obviously, stupidity and lust are a deadly combination. Had she loved me, she would have never put me in that situation in the first place. I let anger, pride, and lust disguised as love blind me from good, sound judgment. My God was truly watching over me that day, and I was not even following His ways then. Unfortunately, our prisons are full of young men who were in the same type of situation as I, but the results were drastically different. Young men, please be smart and take the time to think before you act.

Before I move on, let me say a few things about the words "I love you." Like I said earlier, these three words are thrown around too freely, but they should not be taken lightly. Love is an amazingly powerful emotion, so the words "I love you" should stand for something. They should not be something you say just because you think it is expected of you. If you don't truly feel it, are not sure, or don't know what it is, don't say it. Back in my earlier years, I had dated this girl for only about two weeks when she told me she loved me. Of course she was waiting for me to say it back. I remember looking at her and thinking, *How in the heck can you love me when you don't even know me?* I didn't respond according to her liking, and she got her feelings hurt. I figured it would have been worse to lie to her and give her false hope in thinking our relationship was at a level it would never be. Keep reading and see how this same type of situation came back to bite me in the butt.

While growing up, Mom always made sure that my siblings and I knew we were very much loved. We didn't have money, but we had love, which is something money can't buy. That reminds me of a country song I once heard that says money can't buy you love, but it will buy you a boat and a truck to pull it. I thought that was pretty funny. In our house, Mom made sure that love was not just something to be assumed; it was verbalized. We even got those "I'm only doing this because I love you" speeches right before or during a butt-whipping. Although, somehow, I don't recall hearing "I love you" when she attacked me after I failed to go pick her up that night. Funny how that works. Since I grew up being told I was loved, it was not difficult for me to do the same to my loved ones. However, I know that it is not commonplace in all homes. I know there are some men who just can't bring themselves to say those words even to their wife and kids. You may have grown up in that same type of environment yourself, but it does not mean you can't change it when you start your family. It's nice to be loved, but it is also nice to be told you are loved. Just make sure you mean it. Saying "I love you" does not make you soft or weak. In fact, I think it shows that you are secure enough within yourself to be able to verbalize your feelings regardless of who's around. So if you are a youngster growing up or one who has grown up, don't make the same mistake. Tell those babies you love them.

Remember how I suggested that you not take the words "I love you" lightly and only say them if you really mean it? Here is an example of how that became real to me. I recall precisely when I first told my wife that I loved her. I planned it all out on how I was going to "wow" this lady. I made a reservation at this really nice restaurant that was located on the top floor of a skyscraper in San Francisco. After dinner as we were taking in the wonderful sights and city lights, I finally got enough courage to tell her that I loved her. She responded by looking deep into my eyes and saying absolutely nothing. That's right—there I was fifty-two floors up having just poured out my heart, and this woman just looks at me. I would say it was awkward, but that doesn't seem to do the moment justice. I didn't push it, nor did I let it spoil an otherwise great evening. I did, however, learn another one of those valuable (and expensive) lessons, and that is that mutual feelings of love are no guarantee. Just as I was free to tell her that I loved her, she was free to respond as she pleased. I eventually wore her down with my overwhelming charm. Okay, what really happened was that she heard my words but wanted more time to see if my actions supported them. I can't help but respect that. I could have let my pride get in the way and said, "The heck with you, woman," leaving her with the check and letting her figure out how she was going to get home. However, that would not have been representative of the character I was trying to develop, and it would have shown that my actions did not support my words. In the end, I would have lost out on the woman God sent just for me.

Last, before we move on to the next emotion, it is important that you know that love is more than just words. *Love* is an action word. If your lips say "I love you" but your actions demonstrate something else, guess which message speaks louder. Yes, I'm saying it again—your actions do indeed speak much louder than anything you could ever say. If you tell your woman or even your kids that you love them but you routinely physically or verbally abuse them, your words aren't going to mean a thing. Regarding children, buying them toys and other items is nice, but nothing says "I love you" to a child like spending quality time with them.

*"For God so loved the world, that He gave His only begotten
Son, that whoever believes in Him shall not perish, but have
eternal life."*

—*John 3:16*

Anger

Okay, enough of that love stuff for now. Let's move on to another extremely powerful emotion that can get you in all kinds of negative situations. Unlike love, which is beautiful but can turn ugly when it goes bad, there is nothing beautiful or appealing about anger. It starts off ugly, and if not controlled quickly, it will only get worse. In fact, I can't think of one positive thing that anger does for you. As we continue to discuss issues that will arise on your journey, you absolutely must be aware of your anger and the negative consequences that come with it. Anger is an emotion on which you can never let your guard down. Once you do, it takes only a few seconds for it to take over a situation.

Anger is a highly charged emotion that, if not controlled, will bring chaos to your life and the lives of those around you. Out-of-control anger is the biggest enemy that can block your ability to make good choices and decisions. It almost always leads to negative results. When you let your anger get the best of you, it is almost impossible to think clearly. This leads to you simply acting or reacting without any real thought to the outcome of the situation.

Anger is a normal and natural human emotion. I am not telling you to not ever get angry. If that were possible, I would write a book on that subject alone. However, since I have yet to master the art of never getting angry, I will continue with what I know. Like I said, to get angry is a natural human emotion, but that is not really what I am talking about. I am talking about out-of-control, out-of-your-mind, act-a-fool kind of anger. Remember, we all get angry, but it is normally your actions that follow as a result of your anger that get you directly to the negative-consequences part of the equation. Just because something makes you angry does not give you the right to act a fool and do as you please. When it comes time to face the consequences, you can't excuse your actions by saying, "I did it because I was mad."

Where I come from, no one ever said, "Little Johnny sure was angry today." It was more like, "Little Johnny was acting a fool today because he got mad again." *Mad* is defined as "being mentally disturbed, deranged, insane, demented." I have seen people who were extremely angry, and the definition of *mad* seemed pretty fitting for them. Personally speaking, I do not wish for my actions while I am angry to be described as "mad." When we let our anger control us, instead of us controlling it, the above definition of *mad* is probably a pretty good description of our behavior. On your journey, it is imperative that you learn that regardless of what has made you angry, you will still be held responsible and accountable for your actions.

It is not unusual to be angry when something bothers you, but the problems come when you don't handle yourself appropriately. I cannot begin to tell you how many men are serving life sentences because of extreme episodes of out-of-control anger that resulted in their taking the lives of others. The obvious negative consequences are that someone lost his or her life and that these men are spending the rest of their lives behind bars. Uncontrolled anger can change your life forever.

The glaring issue with being out of control is that either you fail to take the time to think or you are unable to think. Another real problem is that while in this state of mind, you are likely to do just about anything. After your anger has subsided, you can think more clearly. Then, you can often see that the issue may not have been as big as it initially appeared; however, by then it may be too late. You are left with the negative consequences of your out-of-control actions.

Perhaps your anger was merited, but more often than not, your actions in an out-of-control state do not justify your level of reaction. All I am saying is that maybe someone did something to really make you angry, but because of your out-of-control state, you went straight to the "mad" level and your actions were way over the top. That is also because, when you are out of control, everything is magnified and blown way out of proportion. After one out-of-control fit, most people are extremely remorseful for their actions, but like I said, by then it may be too late. Saying you're sorry may seem like nothing but hollow, meaningless words by then.

Sometimes, saying "I am sorry" can get you forgiveness and maybe another chance. However, when people hear it constantly, after a while it doesn't mean anything. Sometimes your actions are so severe that your apology, which may really be sincere, means little or nothing, and you must still deal with the consequences of your actions. These are the situations you must avoid at all costs. Plenty of things in life are out of our control, but our actions as a result of extreme anger are not among them. Control it before it controls you. Get angry if you must, but avoid the "mad" state of mind and start thinking clearly. Otherwise, you might do something you will most likely regret.

"Be angry, and yet do not sin; do not let the sun go down on your anger".

—*Ephesians 4:26*

Back in chapter 3, we talked about doing a sincere self-analysis when looking for those potential flaws in the foundation of your character. We talked about being brutally honest with yourself during this self-inspection period. During this self-analysis, you can also try to determine what it is that gets you to the point of your anger being out of control (your triggers). You need to know what triggers get you to that point where you are no longer thinking, to the point that your rage blinds you and you are not able to see yourself moving fast down the road to negative consequences. If you know your triggers and see that you are heading down the road of bad results, you have a better chance of immediately taking the exit off of that road.

During the anger self-analysis, it is imperative to be honest with yourself, not only to identify the triggers themselves but what makes them your triggers. Why does something make you so angry to the point that you are out of control? It is during this period of real self-reflection that you may have to admit to yourself that the real problem may be you and not always the actions of others. It is much easier to blame our negative actions on others when we should first admit that we have issues and, second, actually take ownership of and accept accountability for those issues.

For as long as I can remember, I have had to deal with anger issues, but I would minimize them by simply saying, "I am just a little hot-headed."

Growing up, I would chalk it up to the "That's just the way I am" excuse. (That's how I know it is just an excuse—I used it too.) It sometimes got me into trouble in high school, but it didn't really reveal its ugly head until I hooked up with my ex-wife and mother of my son. For starters, this woman and I had absolutely no business ever getting married. We were two young and strong-willed individuals who didn't really have a lot in common.

When we would get into arguments, which was often, trying to reason was a total waste of time. The more I tried to talk to her, the more frustrated I became. And the angrier I became, the angrier she got. Now all we had was two hot-headed fools talking in circles. It was much more yelling than it was talking. We would talk over each other. As time went on, things got worse. I began taking out my frustrations by punching walls. *Life Lesson*: This form of frustration release is not very smart for three good reasons. First, it is not anger control by any means. Second, you have to pay for the damage to the walls. And third, once, I hit a very solid wooden door. Let's just say the door won and my nearly fractured wrist lost big time. My wrist was hurting like crazy, and to top it off I felt really stupid. It didn't help that my ex got a good laugh out of that one. I learned my lesson and didn't do that again. As the saying goes, "Stupid is as stupid does."

As the years went on, our relationship got worse. We were married five years, and there is no doubt it would have ended sooner had it not been for me spending a lot of time away from home at sea while in the navy. I also did not want my son growing up without his father and mother living in the same home. However, toward the end, it became apparent that if we stayed together, one of us was probably going to be dead and the other was going to be in prison. Neither of those options appealed to me. That option also served no positive purpose for the kids (she had a daughter from a previous relationship). After years of pent-up anger and resentment on both of our parts, we got into a really big fight over only God knows what. Things finally got to the point of no return, and that was the last day that we lived together as husband and wife.

Remember a bit earlier when I talked about knowing your triggers? Well, you had better know them because sometimes others know them better than you do and will activate them if you let them. The problem is not always others' "pressing my buttons" but my not recognizing them first and doing something about it. Know your triggers and do everything in your power to avoid those situations because nothing good can come from them.

"Do not associate with a man given to anger; or go with a hot-tempered man. Or you will learn their ways and find a snare for yourself."
—*Proverbs 22:24–25*

I remember thinking about why my ex and I weren't getting along. I don't think it was just any one reason but several issues. Like I said, we were both young and very strong-willed individuals. I guess the inability to communicate didn't help things. Our relationship was at a huge disadvantage from the start because it was never built on a solid foundation. So when the winds blew, which it did a lot, our house could not stand.

I learned a lot about myself as a result of the failed relationship with my son's mother, specifically in the area of anger management. I learned what my triggers were during that time in my life. They were primarily related to the frustration that grew from my inability to defuse matters between us with communication. The inability to communicate effectively increased my frustration levels, which in turn caused small matters to appear larger than they were and real problems to feel insurmountable. Identifying my issues helped me to avoid those types of incidents in the future. These revelations did help me in my personal growth and future relationships, but it was much too late to save the one between my ex and me.

I may not be an expert in the field of anger management or anger-related disorders, but I know what I learned from some hard-earned life experience. That was another one of those hard lessons life had dealt me. I also had to admit some very unflattering things about myself. I learned that when I am in a "mad" state, I surrender control, and I hate not being in control of myself. I have learned that sometimes people can and will purposely aggravate you so they can sit back and watch you spin out of control. They only have control if you give it to them.

Uncontrolled anger issues have been the downfall of many men. You need to identify your issues so you can recognize oncoming troubles and get out of the way. Only in the comic books can a person have extreme anger-management issues like the Hulk and use them to his benefit. He would get mad, bust out of his clothes, and cause havoc and chaos. Then after he cooled off, he would turn back into the nice doctor guy. Of course, by then he had caused a whole lot of damage. In real life, uncontrolled anger hurts you and those around you. In real life, uncontrolled anger puts people in hospitals, prisons, and graves.

There is nothing easy about admitting you have a problem. However, if you don't admit it and, more importantly, do something about it, you and everyone around you will suffer. Identify it, admit it, and control it before it controls you. Learning to manage your anger issues is a slow, on-going process. It is also something you will have to manage and stay on top of for a lifetime. I am nowhere near the angry youngster I was, but I am still human and can still have my moments. Learn to avoid people and situations that will try to lead you down the road of being out of control. Since you are responsible and accountable for your actions, it would be in your best interest to control yourself. Sometimes avoidance is in the form of your holding your tongue and not arguing. Sometimes it means walking away from a fight, or staying away from certain people altogether may be your best bet. Do what you have to do to stay away from the out-of-control "mad" zone.

> "A quick-tempered man acts foolishly, and a man of evil devices is hated."
> —*Proverbs 14:17*

While we have only talked about the powerful emotions of love and anger in this chapter, there are many more. However, those two can get you in the most trouble if not handled correctly. We will speak about a few more emotions and feelings that can most assuredly affect you moving forward.

Happiness

After discussing the complexities of love and anger, talking about being happy should be a piece of cake. However, like love, being happy means a lot of different things to different people. It is also a very fluid emotional state, meaning that what you think makes you happy at fifteen or twenty years old may not be the same thing that makes you happy when you are thirty or forty. Some people will say that being happy is simply the absence of sadness in their lives. Some would say that finding true romantic love and spending the rest of their lives together is happiness, while others may say that having lots of money, a fancy house, or a big shiny car defines happiness to them. The list is endless because it is based on individual perception. I have asked some people what they want in life, and the response is often something along the lines of, "I just want to be happy." When I asked further what exactly that meant, I was told, "I'm not sure, but I want it."

Since we all have different and distinct personalities, we tend to define happiness differently. As an individual, you will need to define for yourself what happiness means to you. After all, before you can seek it out, you must first know what it is you are looking for. Then you need to ask yourself why your definition of happiness will make you happy. I am of the opinion that to answer that question, you need to know who you are first. Until then, because you lack foundation, self-identity, and focus, your way of thinking is like a sailboat at sea without a sail. Until you know who you are, you will not know what you want. And happiness will be elusive and always appear just out of your grasp.

I have learned that if you solely base your level of happiness on material possessions like homes, cars, and money, you will be standing on a shaky foundation because "stuff" can be taken away from you at any moment. I am not saying those possessions are not nice to have and can bring a smile to your face. Just know that material possessions can be fleeting, here today and gone tomorrow. They should not be the top priority in your life. If you do make them your highest priority, does it mean that once the possessions are gone you cease to exist or have a purpose? You have to answer that one for yourself.

I was watching the news one day, and the reporter was talking to a family in Oklahoma who had just lost everything they owned to a massive tornado. The camera panned to the devastation behind the husband and wife. What stuck in my mind was that when the camera returned to the wife, she had a smile on her face. She wasn't crazy, but she was grateful to God that their lives had been spared in the chaos. That is an excellent example of placing your happiness in more than possessions. She knew firsthand that possessions could be replaced, but their lives could not.

Here is something else to think about. Some of the rich and famous people the media call stars, who have all the possessions they could ever want, are some of the unhappiest people in the world. I think that is because they believed that once they became rich and famous, happiness would surely follow. When it didn't, they sought it in meaningless sexual relationships, alcohol, drugs, and other self-destructive outlets.

I have learned that happiness must come from within. Without it, you are solely dependent on someone else making you happy. Just as possessions can come and go, so do people in your life. If your total happiness is based on a person and that person's role in your life comes to an end, you will be very disappointed, unhappy, and standing on a very unstable foundation. So instead of allowing another person to be totally responsible for your happiness, you should take ownership of your own happiness. Let others add to your happiness instead of making them the sole source of it.

I strongly believe that your outlook or attitude plays a major role in life. Without a doubt, how you think will have a direct impact on your life. If you see everything in life with a negative tinting, trust me—your life can't help but be negative. It's not because everything in your life is bad but because you *think* everything in your life is bad. And negativity will be all you will see. With this type of attitude toward life, good things could be right in front of you, but due to your outlook, you will look right past them to find the bad. In contrast, having a positive outlook will help you see the good things in life. That does not mean that bad things don't happen to positive people. It just means that they refuse to see life in only a negative view. The lady who lost everything to a tornado is a good example of this concept.

To be happy, you must choose to be happy and not live your life in misery. If you seek nothing but negativity in life, I promise, you will find it. Positive people tend to have gratitude and appreciation for the things that they have in life rather than just focusing on the things they don't have. The power of the mind and your attitude is an amazing thing. When you find yourself in darkness, never cease to search out the light.

I have learned that life is not all about being happy. It is more about bringing joy and happiness to the lives of others. Contrary to the beliefs of some, life is not all about you. You cannot always be a taker and never a giver. You can't always be the one to be served. You need to serve as well.

As I have traveled my journey, I have learned that while I was in search of happiness, I was actually in search of peace within myself and purpose of being. For me, that didn't start until I stopped running from and started running toward God. I found out that life was much more than me and my happiness. It was about me using my talents, gifts, and abilities for His kingdom and the service to others. Once I realized I was a part of something much more important and bigger than myself, I could better see my purpose.

Like I said, the happiness I thought I was looking for was actually peace within myself. For me, that only came as I started to have a real relationship with God. Then and only then did I finally stop getting in my own way and begin letting God mold me into the man He intended for me to be. Being at peace with what God had in store for me brought contentment and real joy. Gone was the constant inner turmoil. I may not know God's entire plan for my life, but I do know He is in charge of my life and that is good enough for me. I may not always know His will, nor do I always do it exactly like I should. However, I do understand His will can't possibly be wrong for me. I know my God has always had my back even when I wasn't doing what I was supposed to be doing. Once I embraced God's plan for me and the importance of His purpose for me to touch lives, then I was able to find deep-rooted joy and happiness.

What makes me happy? It's things like writing this book for the opportunity to hopefully get you to think about your actions, talking to young people, and sharing my experiences to help them not make the same mistakes I made. Happiness, joy, and contentment for me come from being the son of my mother, husband to my wife, father to my children, and Papi to my grandchildren. It was a long, hard road to get to this point due to my stubbornness. God had to send me through some things so I could recognize and appreciate His many blessings in my life. I guess you could say the reason I could never find happiness was because I was looking in the wrong places. What I have inside me can only be given by God.

Trust me, I understand that life can and will send hardships my way that may temporarily take away my smile but not the peace in my heart. God's peace is eternal and is based on His grace, not my goodness;

therefore, it cannot be taken away. You can give away your peace and joy by refusing to accept it, but it cannot be taken away.

> *"For to a person who is good in His sight, He has given wisdom and knowledge and joy, while to the sinner He has given the task of gathering and collecting so that he may give to one who is good in God's sight. This too is vanity and striving after the wind."*
>
> *—Ecclesiastes 2:26*

Fear

Fear is also an extremely powerful emotion. Some of you super-tough guys will say that you are not afraid of anything. While I am not calling anybody a liar, it would be a pretty safe bet to say we are all afraid of something, even if we choose not to admit it. Some have a fear of dying or the death of a loved one. Some even fear life or the thought of being alone. Some have a fear of failure or the expectations that may come along with success. Just as certain things make people happy, certain things scare us. What is important to know is that we all have fears. Some may not be able to admit that they have them to others, but deep inside they know what scares them.

Honestly speaking, I think some fear is good for you. Just try not to let it incapacitate or freeze you, making it impossible to live life to the fullest. A good type of fear is the kind that stops most people from jumping off of a bridge just for the heck of it. I say *most people* because some folks are thrill seekers and live for extreme sports, like bungee jumping, skydiving, or swimming with sharks for fun. Even these folks have fears, perhaps of things that don't scare you. This is just another example of how different people are. The fear of going to prison stopped me from doing a lot of unwise things.

Here is a personal example of not letting fear freeze you from living your life. A long time ago, I was in a serious relationship with a woman I did love. I think she loved me too, just not enough to not play me like a bass guitar. Now after this relationship finally fell apart (after eleven years this time), I had some serious fears. The first was the fear that I couldn't pick the right woman to save my life. Now this was a legitimate fear because my track record in the area of finding the right woman was not very good at all. My selection process needed to be seriously revised. Apparently, just because a female is cute and has a big butt and big boobs, she is not necessarily the right woman. I sure wish someone would have told me that a long time ago. So that's why I am telling you that now.

My other fear was that, because I now had some serious trust issues, I would never be able to love again. So there I was once again, doing another serious, honest self-analysis to see what I was doing wrong. It took a while, but I realized that I needed to do a complete overhaul of my "pick a woman" criteria. I also had to overcome my fear of trusting and of being in love. I knew that I had something to offer, and my heart was very capable of loving again. I just needed to find the right lady. I initially had the mind-set that I was never going to love again, and I was just going to dog as many women as possible. That mind-set didn't last long because that is a victim mentality, and I don't do "victim" well. It also didn't go along with the character expectations I had for myself. Besides, with that negative outlook, all it would do is hurt me in the long run by ensuring I would never love again. So I decided to not let my fear stop me from living or loving.

A reality in life is that you cannot control most aspects of it. There are no sure-fire guarantees, so there will always be areas and outcomes that will be unknown to you. However, that is not a good enough excuse to not live your life. I have said it before and I will say it again: Since you don't have ultimate control, I suggest you control the things you can and prepare the best you can for everything else.

Last year I was talking to my then eight-year-old grandson, and he was telling me about his fear of heights. I told him that sometimes in life we just have to face our fears and move on. Perhaps it was a little too heavy of a conversation for an eight-year-old boy, but in my defense, I told him it was okay to be afraid of things like snakes and spiders. About a month later, he came to me and said, "Papi, I faced my fear, and it wasn't that bad after all." Sometimes in life, we just need to face our fears to move on. Many times in my career, I had to accept challenges that scared me to death. Fortunately for me, I also feared letting opportunities go by simply because I was scared.

When facing your fears, you have to be honest and ask yourself what the real reason is that you are not doing something. Are you just using fear as an excuse to not step up to the challenge, like I did when I was asked to be chief? Don't let fear be the reason you choose to not even try. Fear of a tiger walking down the street and the fear to move outside your comfort zone are not the same thing.

My grandson learned a valuable lesson regarding facing his fears; now all I have to do is get the little hardhead to stop climbing on *top* of the monkey bars. As a side note, a lesson that was reinforced through that interaction with my grandson is that our children are always listening and watching us even when we don't think they are, so love them enough to set good examples.

Last, uncontrolled or unconquered fears can lead to other life-draining emotions and feelings. Some examples include fear of heartbreak, which can lead to the inability to love, like it almost did to me. That same fear of heartbreak can lead to loneliness, inability to trust or forgive, bitterness, and doubt in yourself. Fear of failure can lead to not living life to its full potential, which can lead to frustration, despair, hopelessness, envy, and resentment of those who do dare to try.

I have learned that you must fight the fear of failure or it will cripple you by not allowing you to even try. If you refuse to at least try, you have already failed. If you try and don't succeed, that doesn't make you a failure. It just means that you were unsuccessful in that particular endeavor at that particular time. *Life Lesson*: Neither you nor anyone else is ever going to be successful at everything you attempt to accomplish. Some of life's best lessons come from being unsuccessful. So make sure you pay attention, learn the valuable lesson, and get back at it. You are never a failure until you stop trying.

> *"The fear of the Lord is the beginning of wisdom, and knowledge of the Holy One is understanding."*
> —*Proverbs 9:10*

Hate

Hate is another one of those powerful feelings that we need to discuss because it always—I repeat, always—leads to negativity. When I talk about hate, I'm talking about the all-consuming hatred one has toward another person, not the "Man, do I hate brussels sprouts" kind of hate. Undoubtedly, some people are just downright evil and may have done some pretty awful things to you. The very sight of these people or even the mention of their name gets you all riled up. These people need to be avoided at all costs before they wake up that anger in you and you do something that brings negative results your way.

Like hate's ugly brother, anger, nothing positive comes from it. The thing about hate is that while it is directed toward someone else, it also hurts you. People you hate may or may not even know you feel that way. And there is a high probability that if they did know, they wouldn't care. That leaves you focusing your energy toward people who are not staying awake at night worried that you may have a strong dislike toward them. You know who gets hurt by hate? If you said "me," then you are correct. The hater, not the hated, gets hurt by hate. You hurt yourself by not moving on from whatever caused you to hate that person in the first place. It takes entirely too much time and energy to dislike someone that deeply—time and energy that you will never get back and that you could use to focus on making you a better person. If you feel that strongly about a person, chances are he or she isn't worth the time or energy anyway.

The other thing you do when you spend all of your time and energy hating is you indirectly give that person power and control over you, and that is the last thing we want to do. Remember, there are enough things in this life that we cannot control, so why would you voluntarily give someone the power and control to make you act in a negative manner?

I'm not going to lie and say that there aren't some people whom I have strongly disliked, like my stepfather before he passed away—okay, maybe a couple of women from past relationships as well, and perhaps a few folks I have run across during my career. However, I can honestly say that I don't hate anyone. I can't say that the reason I don't have hate in my heart is that I am some special kind of loving guy. The truth is that this is an area

God has been working on in me for a while. There is no way I could have made this statement during my angry years.

It was not until relatively recently that I realized that hate did nothing but make me feel ugly inside. God's love inside of me must be pushing the ugliness out. I figured that if Jesus could ask God to forgive the very same people who had just nailed Him to the cross, who was I to hate anyone?

A few years ago, I ran into a man for whom I had a super powerful dislike because he had done some pretty foul things to my family. Before seeing him, I had been praying for God to take away the ugly thoughts I had toward him. So when I saw him, I approached him, said hello, and even shook his hand. What was truly amazing was that I honestly didn't desire to break his neck anymore. That was a personal victory for me in a major way. Again, it showed that God truly was working on me because if I had seen him a few years earlier, I would have reacted very differently. Hate is all consuming and not worth the time or energy. Hate is blinding and can seriously affect your ability to think clearly. You know nothing good ever comes when you are in that state of mind. Do not give others that kind of power over you.

> *"But the one who hates his brother is in darkness and walks in darkness, and does not know where he is going because the darkness has blinded his eyes."*
>
> *—1 John 2:11*

I have given you a lot to digest mentally regarding emotions and feelings. What I want you to take away from this chapter is, of course, the awareness of the emotions themselves but, more importantly, how they can affect you.

Try not to make important decisions while you are either too emotionally high or too emotionally low. You will make your best decisions when you are somewhere in the middle. So that means that if you are floating on the clouds of love or low in the basement, be aware of your present state of mind and make your decisions accordingly. Both states of mind can give you false information when making serious decisions. When you are over the moon happy, you will tend to see things as you like rather than as they are. If you are too low, you will tend to make things out to be a lot worse than they actually are. Always avoid making big, life-altering decisions in either frame of mind. Find that stable middle ground before making those big decisions.

Personally, I try to incorporate extra thought in my words and actions when I am in a frustrated, agitated, or angry frame of mind. I know that when I am like that, things appear much worse than they are. Therefore, I know it is very important that I step back, breathe, and try to get a hold of myself before I say or do something that could lead to negative consequences.

When I was chief and one of the agents did something that initially appeared totally contrary to our policy and procedures, I knew I needed to take a moment before I spoke to the manager of the agent because I knew there was a good chance that, initially, I probably didn't have the complete story. Even if it was later determined that the agent did indeed violate policy, I still needed to take the time to digest the situation before I had to reprimand this person. That helped me to focus on correcting the problem and not just react out of anger.

The bottom line is that emotions not only affect how you feel, but they also affect how you think and subsequently act. Know yourself and make changes as needed. Know your triggers and avoid people who can activate those triggers. Know that negative emotions are going to accompany life's hardships, so be forewarned and not surprised when they come. When they do come, ride them out without doing something silly that you may regret because it will eventually get better. Know that you are not the first or the last person to experience these emotions. Last, the saying that real men don't cry is a lie. If something hurts, instead of trying to hold everything in, a good cry is a good, healthy release. Find a place to be alone and let it go. Don't hold all that stuff in.

> *"The wisdom of the sensible is to understand his way, but the foolishness of fools is deceit."*
> —*Proverbs 14:8*

CHAPTER 5

RELATIONSHIPS

As I get older and hopefully wiser, it becomes abundantly clear that life is so much more about the people in our lives than about the things in it. As I mentioned in the last chapter, there is nothing wrong with wanting material possessions. Just don't make them your life because, in the end, it really is just stuff—stuff that can be taken away just as easily as it was acquired. At the end of your life, what's going to matter the most is not the things you had but the relationships you established along your journey. What people meant in your life and, even more importantly, what you meant in the lives of others is what really matters.

You will have many types of relationships in life. On your journey, you will learn and understand that there are very few people who will be in your life for long periods of time. Most people are going to be in your life for only a relatively short period. I say *relatively* because your perspective on time is dependent on your stage in life. Growing up, I couldn't wait to go from nine years old to ten so I could be in the double digits. And then came sixteen, when I could drive. Then I was eighteen, when I was legally considered an adult, and of course twenty-one, when I could legally purchase alcohol. Once I got into my twenties and started working in the prisons, I couldn't wait to get some time under my belt so I could stop being called a rookie or "fish," as they called it inside. I always assumed they called us that because the veteran officers and inmates could smell our newness a mile away. After getting in some time, I couldn't wait to get promoted. Once the promotions start, you soon begin to start thinking about how many years you have left before retirement. Time really is fleeting, so don't waste it.

I say all of this because when you are young, you tend to think you have all the time in the world to get things right in your life. You can also have the tendency to think you are invincible and that you are going to live forever. I will tell you that neither is true; in reality, life is quite short.

The sooner you grasp that concept, the sooner you will understand and learn to appreciate the value of positive relationships in your life. Just in case you have never heard this before, let me be the first to tell you that tomorrow is not promised. I suggest you learn to appreciate today and the good people in it.

Some of this may have you thinking, *What the heck is this old guy talking about?* I am okay with that because not everything in this book is intended for you to grasp totally right now. It is intended to be, as the subtitle indicates, "a resource," something you can come back to as you continue into the different stages of your journey. Just stick with me as one day you will say, "Oh, that's what that dude was talking about."

As you progress on your journey, you will learn that as you get older (and hopefully wiser), the way you think changes. As I write this book at fifty-two years old, I'm at a point where I am reflecting on my life choices, decisions, and lessons learned, as well as the people who have come and gone in my life—not only the positive but the negative as well. I have learned that you can learn something from just about everybody you encounter in your life. If you acquire the positive character traits we talked about earlier, it should also be your desire to pass on something positive to the lives of those you encounter along the way.

A few people in my life have been there for a long time, but most have come and gone. There is a poem (specific author unknown) that talks about people coming into your life, or you into theirs, titled, "Reason, Season, Lifetime." I have learned this to be very true. Sometimes, people come into your life to help you get through extremely challenging times. These people seem to be heaven sent because it seems like they just appear out of nowhere for the "reason" of helping you get through a storm in life. Sometimes, the reason people come into your life is to show you that all things in life are not as bad as you think, and you share a time of complete joy and happiness. However, sometimes for reasons not completely known to us, people leave from our lives after what we feel is a short period of time. These are the folks who were in our lives for a particular reason; however, it was not intended to be for the long haul. These are the people who are in your life for only a "season." The reason and season folks' arrivals and departures may not seem sensible to us, and it can often feel extremely unfair when they leave. Life itself can seem extremely unfair and difficult at times, and that's because it is. Fairness and ease of life are not always how things work in our journeys. Since you are not in control of all things in your life, learn to appreciate the positive things gained, learned, and experienced from our reasons and seasons. Just because things did not go the way you wished they had, don't turn positives into negatives by focusing on the departure more than the experiences shared while they were in your life.

Before I move on, you should know that not all reasons and seasons are initially positive. What I mean is that sometimes people come into your life and bring nothing but pain and sorrow with them. These folks are also there for a reason; however, unfortunately, the lessons learned are the difficult ones. These people may be there to help prepare you for greater things later in life. When they come into your life, just hope and pray it is only for a short season. Pay attention and learn the lessons life has to give you. No matter who you are, you will endure challenging times, so you might as well take something positive from it. It can either help you prepare for the future or help you appreciate all the more when the good comes your way. When a "reason" is coming to an end or a "season" has passed, don't fight it—just as you can't fight winter giving way to spring or fall to winter because it is just the nature of things. Embrace it while you can.

As I mentioned, I have had some serious challenges in my romantic relationships in the past. However, I learned that the reason and season (positive and negative) women in my past all had a part in preparing me for my present wife and soulmate. I feel that, had I not experienced and endured (through God's grace) past hardships, I would have never recognized or been able to truly appreciate just how amazing of a person she really is. Like I tell my sons and will tell my grandsons, "I did not just get here to my present place in life. I had to go through some things." Learn the lessons and prove that you have learned them by applying them to your life.

The reasons and seasons help you prepare and appreciate the people that come into your life and are there for a "lifetime." Lifetime people are the ones you need to make sure you recognize and value for the true treasures they are. These folks know all your good and not-so-good points and love you regardless. Never take for granted the role these people play in your life and the role you play in theirs.

Along your journey, you may have friends right now whom you may think will be there your whole life. That may be true in some situations, but it simply is not the norm. Life will get in the way, and for whatever reason, you simply grow apart and move in different directions. You will learn that this is the case many times along your journey. So don't take it personally. Just try and remember that it is the cycle of life and enjoy them while you can. I think when these cycles occur, it will just make you truly appreciate the gift of the lifetime folks you do have in your life. Not only do you know the good and bad about each other, but you also get to watch each other grow. These are the people you need to remind you to appreciate the good things in your life because they were there when things were much worse. They also remind you to never forget where you came from, and they help you maintain or find humility. Lifetimers will be your biggest fans and sincerely celebrate your victories. They will also be there when life has you beat down and you doubt your ability to take another step. Recognize and, with much gratitude, appreciate your lifetime relationships for they are truly a blessing and should never be seen as anything other than a wonderful gift.

> *"There is an appointed time for everything, and there is a time for every event under heaven."*
> —*Ecclesiastes 3:1*

Before we start talking about specific relationships, let's talk a bit about a few key elements I believe are vital to success regardless of the type of connection. Real relationships not only need to be appreciated and valued; they also need to be nurtured. A gardener or a farmer wouldn't feed their flowers or crops just anything and still expect to get beautiful flowers or healthy vegetables. You will get what you put into a relationship. If you want good things to come from your relationships, you are going to need to put good things into it. You can't treat people like crap and in turn expect them to treat you like royalty. If you recall earlier, I told you that life is not just about you. You can't only be a taker and never a giver. When I talk about being a giver, I am not talking about material things or possessions. I am talking about giving of yourself to encourage and lift others up instead of tearing them down. Sometimes all that takes is a sincere smile or a word of encouragement. Don't always try to make things all about you and your needs. I know plenty of people who do things for others only if they get something in return. I call that the "what's in it for me" mentality. It is a selfish mind-set, and it has no place in the establishment and maintenance of a healthy relationship.

A hard truth in life is that just because you give the best of yourself in a relationship, the same will not automatically be given in return. That is something you simply cannot control. However, it is up to you if you want to stay connected to that relationship. The mentality I would like you to have is that you give of yourself because that is what you expect from yourself. I refuse to let the actions of others lower my self-expectations. If I find myself in relationship that is one-way, caustic, and detrimental to my well-being, then I assume this person is in my life for a negative reason and, therefore, a short season. Of course, many elements go into healthy and wholesome relationships, but honesty, trust, and respect are vital to all healthy relationships.

Honesty

For any relationship to have a chance of success, it must be established in mutual honesty. Anything based on fabrication and lies cannot survive. The thing about building a relationship on lies is that eventually the lies will reveal themselves and the truth will come to light. Just keep in mind that honesty is not always warm and fuzzy. In fact, honesty may reveal some downright unflattering details. I prefer the truth even if it may hurt me; at least I know what I am dealing with. Then I am free to make my decision on how I wish to proceed. Anything founded and based on a lie cannot succeed. Be honest with others and expect honesty in return. If you recall, honesty is one of those character traits we talked about, so make it a part of your foundation. I know not everyone is honest, but what does that have to do with you? Even if everyone around you is dishonest, that does not give you an excuse to stray from the truth.

I have learned that honesty truly is the best policy. The truth is easy to remember. Once you head down the road of lies, it never ends with just one lie. You will continue to lie to cover the other lies. A liar has to focus too much energy to remember all the lies and who he told them to. Honesty is so much easier, and it comes with peace of mind because you are free from the stress and pressure of your lie coming to light. Deep down inside, all liars know that one day the truth will come out. The bottom line is that if you want good relationships, be sure to include honesty in the base of the foundation.

"A truthful witness saves lives, but he who utters lies is treacherous."

—*Proverbs 14:25*

Trust

Just as it is important that a strong relationship is based on honesty, it is also important that there is mutual trust. It is vital that both parties in a relationship have confidence that the other is truly who they say they are and can be relied on to do what they say they are going to do. If you only remember one thing about trust, please make it this: Trust is hard earned but easily lost. The gaining of trust is not achieved overnight. It is a process that can sometimes take years. However, it can be lost in the blink of an eye.

Along with having someone trust you with their emotions is the responsibility of not violating that trust. If you truly value a relationship, it is worth your effort to ensure that the other person knows you can be trusted not to bring them physical or emotional harm, you are going to be a man of your word, and you will do what you said you would do. A classic violation of trust in romantic relationships is when one person commits to being intimate with only the other person but is discovered to be cheating. In this situation, you may have spent plenty of time and effort to gain the other person's trust. The other person put their trust in you, let their guard down, and let you into their world. However, when it is discovered that you aren't the person you claimed to be, everything you have done positively to gain their trust is gone, or at the very least it is in question. Depending on the other person, you may get another chance to prove yourself, but then again you may not. Also, remember that your trustworthiness—or lack thereof—is a strong statement to your character.

While I gave the example of trust lost in a romantic scenario, it can happen in any relationship. Throughout my life, people have violated the trust I had in them. I have also violated the trust that others may have had in me. It didn't take much for me to realize that I didn't like being on either side of those experiences. However, when someone violates your trust, it is the result of that person making a choice and deciding to act on it. In my case, the consequence was that they lost my trust. While it does in fact hurt, there is not anything I could have done to prevent it because I am not in control of the actions of others. It is up to you to determine how you will react to the violation. I can't tell you to give the person another chance as that is between you and your heart. I can tell you that the only person who was perfect is Jesus. Trust me, there will be many times in your life when you will seek forgiveness, so you may want to learn how to forgive on occasion.

Being on the receiving end of lost trust hurts, but what hurts even more to me was when I was the person who violated the trust. In that situation, I was the one in control of my actions and totally responsible for the pain and suffering I brought to the other person. That's what happened when I didn't come to my mother's rescue when she needed me. What hurt me was that I could see in her eyes that I had violated the trust that she had in me. One bad decision immediately damaged a lifetime of gaining her trust. Since I was her son, she didn't cut me loose or kick me out of the house, but there then existed something in our relationship that had never existed before—and that was doubt. She had doubt that I was the son she hoped and that I claimed to be. To me that was nearly unbearable, and I would spend quite some time trying to regain her lost trust.

It's pretty much a guarantee while on your journey that you will put your trust in someone and it will be violated. There is also a very good chance that you will violate the trust someone has put in you as well. These are events you will face in life. They are painful, yes, but it is one of those hard lessons you must endure and hopefully learn from.

Just because your trust has been violated does not mean you shouldn't ever trust again, but it does mean you need to learn from the experience. *Life Lesson:* Not everyone you will encounter along your journey is worthy of your trust. In general, I am not a very trusting person, so it takes time to gain my trust. However, once you gain my trust and I lower my guard, you are now in my very small inner circle. I, in turn, will do everything in my power not to violate your trust in me. Can these people I choose to trust and let into my world hurt me? Absolutely, but I am not going to let that stop me from doing my part to grow and maintain lifetime relationships.

If and when you find that you have violated the trust of another, try not to beat yourself up too badly. Then again, if it doesn't bother you, then it's time for one of those character evaluations we talked about earlier. Even if the other person chooses not to forgive you (remember, it is their choice), find a way to forgive yourself and ensure that you have learned the hard lesson. Again, the best way to prove that you learned a lesson is to not repeat the offense. The last thing I will say about trust (for now) is that it is very much an action word. You do not gain trust by telling someone how trustworthy you are. You do it by letting your actions show you are worthy of their trust.

> *"In God, I have put my trust; I shall not be afraid. What can man do to me?"*
>
> —*Psalm 56:11*

Respect

Respect is another one of those words that is thrown around, a lot like *love* and *happy*. A person who is well respected in his or her field of expertise is looked upon favorably because of what he or she does, like a star professional athlete. Another form of respect can come as a result of the contributions someone has given to the world, as in the case of Dr. Martin Luther King Jr. While he was respected for his leadership, it was his character that set him apart. There is absolutely nothing wrong with being respected for your accomplishments in a certain activity or career, but never forget to strive to be respected for your character as it will be your character that will speak louder about who you are long after accomplishments have come and gone. Let's say you desire to be respected for being the greatest athlete of all time, but your character is less than it should be. What do you think your legacy will be? It could very well be that people will say you were indeed the greatest athlete to ever live but you were a terrible person. I know that is not how I want to be remembered. Seek to be respected for who you are, not just for what you do.

Unfortunately, there is another form of misidentified respect that usually has negative meaning among young men of color. You will hear it used as an excuse or misguided reasoning for making a poor decision, like, "I did what I had to do because he disrespected me." This form of respect is nothing more than a poor excuse for making a poor choice—and an even poorer decision to act. I cannot even begin to think how many young men we have in our prisons and cemeteries because of the distorted notion of what respect is.

Respect is defined as "Esteem for or a sense of the worth or excellence of a person, a personal quality or ability, for something considered as a manifestation of a personal quality or ability." When we talk about respect in this chapter, we will focus on what it means in a relationship.

In a foundationally sound relationship, along with honesty and trust, you must have a mutual respect for each other. Just as the definition stated, "Esteem for or a sense of the worth or excellence of a person," if you have esteem (or value) for another person, it should show itself in the way you treat that person. If I tell you that I have the utmost respect for you but routinely lie to you or about you, then my actions don't reflect my words. For example, if I told you that I respect you and value your opinion but every time you tried to share sound advice with me, I told you to shut up because you don't know what you are talking about, my words would not support my claim of respect for you. *Respect* is another one of those "show me, don't tell me" action words.

If you value or have true respect for someone, it should strongly influence how you treat that person. If you value something—let's say a vehicle—you take excellent care of it and maintain it properly. You also make sure it stays clean and not allow others to damage it. So if you would do that for possession, why would you not do that and much more to show your respect to another person whom you say you value?

Just as trust must be nurtured, so must respect. Respect is also hard earned and easily lost. Earlier in the book, I mentioned that respect is earned, not just demanded. If you want respect in life, then you may want to make a habit of giving it. Carry yourself in a manner worthy of respect. If you find yourself in a relationship that is lacking in mutual respect, meaning you are giving it but not receiving it in return, then it is time to reevaluate the level of commitment and sincerity in that relationship. You may also want to ask yourself the hard question, "Am I being respectful, and are my actions worthy of respect?"

Respect in real relationships is really not that complex. If you have true respect for another person, you will care for their well-being and do everything in your power to not cause them harm. You will lift them up, not discourage them. You will be there for them in good and bad times. You won't lie to them. You won't beat or cheat on them. You will be dependable by doing what you said you would do. You will show them by your actions, not just your words, that you value and respect them. These are the things that lifetime relationships are made of.

It's a funny thing, proclaiming to have respect for others when your actions do not reinforce who you say you are. It is your actions that reveal your true character, and in the end, by not giving respect, you wind up disrespecting yourself.

Last, and this is a real sore spot I have specifically among my people, is the lack of respect shown to black women by calling them something other than their names. Our women are not "bitches and hoes." If you feel violated and compelled to address black females as such, then obviously you need to look within and ask yourself why you feel it necessary to demean the givers of physical life in such a profane manner. If that is the norm where you are from, then perhaps you need to change your environment and your frame of mind. Black women have done a tremendous job in the face of great adversity, and they have often done it alone. The least we can do as their men is to protect and respect them.

"A good name is more desirable than great wealth, favor is better than silver and gold."

—Proverbs 22:1

Family

There is a saying that goes, "You can pick your friends but not your family." Now, you can take this statement as a positive or a negative, but I always just took it at face value. To me, it means you have a choice about who you call a friend, but like it or not, you are simply born into your family. Good or bad, "you got what you got."

There is something to be said regarding blood relatives—you know, the kind who will have your back no matter what. Growing up in Stockton, we didn't have a big family. It was primarily Mom, my sister, and my baby brother, who came way later. I have another brother who is between my sister and my baby brother, but the only thing this brother and I had in common was that we shared the same mother. He was always out of control and often away in some type of facility. As we grew up, whenever we did run into each other by chance, it was only a matter of minutes before we got into a confrontation. The main issue between us has always been that he idolized his father, my stepfather, who could do no wrong in my brother's eyes. As you can see, this was no minor difference of opinion. Whenever the fighting between my mom and stepdad would start up, my brother would always root for his dad to beat my mother. I doubt we ever saw eye to eye on anything. My brother is the type who thinks that everything that has ever gone wrong in his life is not his fault but somebody else's.

My brother is a classic example of not being able to pick your family. Neither of us would have chosen the other as family, nor as a friend for that matter. Now, on my real father's side of the fence, there is a very large family; however, I didn't know them as they were mostly in the Los Angeles area. I began meeting them later as I became an adult. I have to admit, it was pretty cool when I found out that I was a part of a bigger family.

Growing up in Stockton, I encountered several large families who always seemed to have an endless supply of brothers, sisters, and cousins. These are the families that you do your best to avoid at all costs because if you fight one, it never ends there. Every time you turn around, there's another one. I did sometimes envy those large clans because they had that built in backup system.

In those big families, I noticed that usually, regardless of whether a family member was in the wrong or the right, they had his or her back no matter what. At first, that may seem cool, particularly when you are young and it involves simple verbal confrontations or fist fights at the worst. However, when you get older, the situations get much bigger and have greater consequences. It seemed like the big families were always coming to the rescue of the same knucklehead family member. So if you find yourself constantly coming to the rescue of the same trouble-finding relative, you have to decide just how far you will go for a person who continually chooses to put him- or herself, and the family, into negative situations.

Just as this family member makes poor choices and frequently finds him- or herself facing negative consequences, I strongly suggest that you think about making better decisions for yourself. Family or not, they don't get to drag you down with them as a result of their continual poor decisions. Remember, we are all responsible for our actions. I am not saying that you should not be there for family, but at the same time, family members should not use their backup as a reason to not make good choices and decisions. Again, this book is not a step-by-step guide on what to do in every situation. It is a resource for thinking before you act. Do what you must; just don't forget the equation before you do it. Just because they are family does not mean the equation is not in effect. Here is some serious food for thought: Going to prison for something you got yourself into is bad enough, let alone getting locked up for someone else's stupidity.

Now, if *you* are that family member who is always in a mess and expecting the family to rescue your butt, please stop dragging your people into your negative consequences. You got yourself in the mess, so stop bringing others down with you. A man is responsible and accountable for his own actions. When making your choices and decisions, please remember that the things you do don't just affect you; they also affect those who care about you as well. Did I mention that life is not all about you? I'm pretty sure I did.

Family can be an amazing support group of people that have the same blood running through their veins. There will be those in your family who you get along with better with than others. There may be some you don't get along with at all, but at the end of the day you can't magically make them not family. Just as in the real world (outside of family), there are people who don't have your best interest in mind, so you have to decide how to proceed from there.

On the flip side, some family members will be your biggest fans in life. They will encourage you and snatch you up when you go astray to get you back on track. Some family members will be there for you when it seems like nothing is going right for you in life to remind you of the type of stock you come from and not allow you to quit at anything. We all have good and bad in our families; embrace the positive and learn to minimize the negative.

We have talked a bit about the family you are born into; now let's discuss the family you create. There comes a time on your journey that you move on from the family you are born into and start to form your extension of the family. While the family you were born into will always be your family, the natural course of life is you grow older, mature, get married, and have children of your own. Notice that I said, "Grow older and mature." Getting older does not automatically mean that you are mature or wiser. Unfortunately, I know men my age and older who are nowhere as mature as their years would have you think. As my mother would always tell us, "There is nothing worse than an old fool."

Okay, back on track. Hopefully, you won't have children until you are mature enough to handle the job of fatherhood. It takes maturity to understand that once you start a family of your own, nothing except God comes before your family. Yes, that includes your mama, daddy, brother, and sister. You will forever be a part of the family into which you were born, but once you take on the responsibility of being a husband and father, your wife and children become your top priority in life.

Taking responsibility for yourself is a big task when you're young, and adding a wife and children to that is huge. This responsibility is not something that you can, or should, take lightly. Like many things in life, if you fail to think and plan, you will find yourself in very unfavorable circumstances. That includes starting a family when you are neither mentally or financially up to the task.

Failure to think and plan can look like this example: You see a woman who has caught your interest, and either you think you are in love, or all you can think about is engaging in sex with her (lust). Let's say the feeling is mutual, and you both decide to engage in sex. She becomes pregnant because neither of you had enough sense to use protection. Either that or you simply didn't care. You probably don't even know what your plans are, but now you have another life coming into the world. Being the male in this relationship, you are expected to "man up" and take care of your child. Unfortunately, this scenario is all too common in our communities. Some young men step up to the plate and grow into responsible fathers, but most run out on their women, leaving them to deal with "the problem" on their own. The cycle continues with our children being raised by single moms doing the best they can by themselves.

Please take the time to think before you act. In our communities, we need more men to step up and be fathers, not "baby daddies." Having a family of your own is such an amazing gift, but it is also very hard work even when you plan it. Unplanned families present a challenge that is that much harder. Life is already naturally difficult, so why make it harder than it has to be?

A plan for a family starts with you knowing who you are. Be honest with yourself. If you know you are not mentally, emotionally, and financially ready to be a father, then don't have unprotected sex. Ideally, I would prefer you not have sex until you are married, as God had intended it to be. I know that is a hard request for most, but I believe if we did more things as God instructed us to do, the world would have a lot fewer problems. Not having sex until you are married reflects planning.

Your plan should also include the right woman to marry and start a family with. The right woman for me may not be the right one for you. Only you can determine the right woman for you, but I highly recommend you first know who you are and what type of man you wish to be. Now, if you wish to have nothing more than someone who is cute with a big butt and boobs, then that's not too hard to find since you are not asking for much. If you think about it, that is not much different than buying a pretty, shiny car and not caring that the engine barely runs. A pretty, shiny car is cool, but the difference maker is the engine, which determines how that car will perform. There is nothing wrong with your woman being sexually attractive to you, but if she is without real thought, morals, and values, she is nothing more than the pretty, shiny car with a weak engine. It might get you across town, but it's only a matter of time until it breaks down on you. Pretty and shiny by itself is only superficial, and it will not last. That is because all the attention went into the outer appearance and not what drives it.

> *"Charm is deceitful and beauty is vain, but a woman who fears the LORD shall be praised."*
> —*Proverbs 31:30*

Now, if you desire to have a woman of intelligence, integrity, morals, and high character, that's going to take some planning. I say *planning* because if you wish to attract that type of mate, then you are going to need to possess those same types of character traits that you are seeking. Trust me, she will be looking for someone with similar traits to complement hers. If you are cool with shallow outer beauty by itself, then a woman with superficial character should be relatively easy to find. Just remember—if you don't expect much, then you won't get much. Please don't forget to ask yourself if this is the type of woman you want to be the mother of your children. If you want to attract someone special, then be someone with special character.

Failure to plan can and will lead to all types of problems. I briefly mentioned that if you aren't ready for fatherhood, then you shouldn't have unprotected sex (without a condom). If you are going to have sex before marriage, then at least be smart about it and wear a condom—not sometimes, not nearly all the time, but every time. Not only does a condom help (not 100 percent) prevent unplanned pregnancy, but it can also save your life. I'm not going to give you a lesson on sexually transmitted diseases (STDs), but I will say that when I was coming up, all we had to worry about was syphilis and gonorrhea, diseases that could pretty much be cleared up with a shot. Today, we are dealing with human immunodeficiency virus (HIV), which causes acquired immune deficiency syndrome (AIDS). HIV/AIDS is no joke and can be mostly avoided, so if you have to have sex, put on a condom. If you fail to plan by not using a condom, not only do you risk becoming a father before you are ready, but you also risk your life and the lives of others. Since being a father is much more than being a sperm donor, which any male with a penis can do, be smart and think before you act.

"He who pursues righteousness and loyalty finds life, righteousness and honor."

—*Proverbs 21:21*

Friends

You may not be able to pick and choose your family, but you sure as heck can pick your friends. Take advantage of the fact that you get to choose your friends and pick them wisely. I suggest that you learn early on that everyone you know is not your friend. Some folks you know are merely acquaintances. I know a whole lot of people, but I am very selective about who I allow in my personal inner circle and call a friend. I am not one who needs a lot of friends to define me. While I wouldn't call myself a loner, I would much rather be alone than be around so-called friends who are insincere. I associate words like *trust, honesty, loyalty*, and *dependability* with the people I call friends.

I am very fond of positive quotes and sayings; we have them all over our home. One plaque we have reads, "The only way to have a friend is to be one." That conveys my feelings about friendship. True friendship should be a two-way street, never forgetting that the world is not just about me. The qualities I desire and expect from the people I call friends are the same things I expect from myself in return.

I just mentioned that trust, honesty, loyalty, and dependability are traits I consider instrumental in the foundation of friendship. If I call you friend, that means that I can trust that you are who you say you are. Therefore, I can trust you with my personal information. If I tell you something, I know that my business isn't going to be spread around the streets. If I call you friend, I know that you will always keep it real with me by being honest, even if the truth may hurt sometimes.

Loyalty and dependability go hand in hand. If I call you friend, I can count on you to support me and know that you are committed to doing what you said you would do. I can depend on you during the good and the bad times. As you can see, I don't take friendship lightly.

These are just a few things I want you to consider before calling someone your friend. If people are truly your friends, they will always have your best interests in mind. They will always want what's best for you. You shouldn't have to worry about a friend being jealous of your accomplishments. They should celebrate them right along with you as if they were their own.

If you have a so-called friend who is jealous of your success or is attempting to get you to do something you know you shouldn't be doing, then that person is not your friend. *Life Lesson:* Sometimes in life, people who you really believe in and trust will let you down and disappoint you. That is because people are not perfect, and on occasion they are plain evil. I always try to look for the positive in everything, even in terribly hard life lessons. When people disappoint you, thank them for revealing their true colors and go your way. It is always better to know who and what you are dealing with than existing with a lie. Like I said before, friendship is a two-way street. If you find yourself envious of a friend's happiness and success, then it's time for you to reevaluate yourself.

Ensure that when you pick your friends you choose like-minded, positive people. It is important that you hang around with people of similar goals and aspirations. An example would be that if you desire to be someone who contributes to your community in a positive manner, then I would not recommend that you hang out with the dudes focused on committing crime. I am not saying that you should act like you are better than others. However, if you have a plan for your life, then it's to your benefit that you associate with people with the same mind-set and ambitions. You can either hurt the feelings of your thug-like acquaintances by saying no, or you can hang with them all the way to jail or prison. It's your call since you are the one who has to deal with the consequences of your decision.

Be very careful regarding the people you choose to hang around because the phrase "guilty by association" is a very real thing. Let's say that for some reason you decide you are going to roll with your thug acquaintances from the neighborhood, and something goes down while you are with them. Even if you didn't do anything, until things get sorted out (if they do), you will be treated as though you are guilty because you were hanging with the thugs. I sure hope you didn't just think, *That's not fair.* I'm pretty sure I have not written anything about life being fair; that is why I keep telling you to think before you act and control the things you can. Fair or not, it is what it is. This is where like-minded friends would keep one another on track and tell you that you have no business rolling around with the thugs. Now, if the thugs are your like-minded friends, it really is time for you to make some drastic lifestyle changes.

> *"He who walks with wise men will be wise, but the companion of fools will suffer harm."*
> —*Proverbs 13:20*

When I speak to young men during youth forums, I always tell them to not only be aware of what's going on with them but be aware of the folks around you as well. Here's a real-life example: You are rolling with some dudes in a car you know you shouldn't be in. One of the guys in the car has a gun that you know nothing about. While you are just cruising, the guy with the gun sees another guy he has a problem with. All of a sudden, the guy with the gun starts shooting and hits the guy he saw. So when the police pull the car over, guess who's going to jail? If you said the guy with the gun, you are right, but don't forget to add everybody else in the car. Yes, everybody in the car is going to jail with a good chance of being charged with attempted murder, or murder if the guy dies. Some of you are thinking, *Surely the guy who pulled the trigger will tell the police he did it and that he acted alone.* Not always, my friend. Our prisons are full of guys doing time for incidents just like this. The shooter was your friend, right? Obviously, he wasn't, or you wouldn't be caught up in this mess. In actuality, he was just a guy you knew from around the way, and he wasn't in the mood to tell on himself that day. The bottom line is that you need to know who you are hanging out with. This is a very avoidable scenario, so avoid it. Pick your friends and associates wisely as your freedom or life may very well depend on it.

The one thing about being a real friend and having friends is that you need to have a clue as to who you are and what expectations you have for yourself. If you don't, you are subject to be like a boat being tossed around because it has no sail. If you don't know who you are (identity), you are subject to major influence by peers you think are your friends. If they are into stupidity and you have not set boundaries for yourself, more than likely you will be doing stupid stuff too. Your inner voice is telling you that this is not something you should be doing, but because you have failed to create an identity of your own, you will tend to flow in the direction of this particular group. Now, not only are you doing stupidity because of your peers, you start doing it because that's what you think is expected of you. Create your own identity early on and choose your friends accordingly.

On your journey, you want to be a man of character, a man who does the right thing even when it's not popular. If you know you are intelligent enough not to be involved in stupidity, then use your good sense to bring the others up, not dumb yourself down to try and fit in. If they don't listen, then that's up to them.

Out of all the people you meet on your life journey, very few will be true friends. When you do come across these people, treasure them and be a blessing to them by being a true friend in return.

> *"A man of too many friends comes to ruin, but there is a friend who sticks closer than a brother."*
> —*Proverbs 18:24*

Marriage

I mentioned the importance of knowing what kind of man you are so that you can find the right woman for you. Let's say you have what you believe is the perfect plan for finding and marrying the woman of your dreams. With your perfect plan in mind, you would think that once you get married and start this new chapter of your life, things should be smooth sailing, right? Well, that's not true because married life is not easy. In fact, sometimes it is just plain hard.

Earlier in the book we talked about being in love and the emotions that go along with it. Well, there is so much more that needs to go into a marriage than the warm and fuzzy feelings you get from the emotions brought on from being in love.

There is much to consider before you make a commitment such as marriage. I'm going to throw out plenty for you to consider before you make that move. However, before I do, let me tell you a very important reason *not* to get married. Do not—I repeat, do not—get married solely based on liking how this particular female makes you feel and not wanting to risk letting her make some other guy feel the same. Too many young men have gotten married for that reason alone. Normally, that thought process is based on sexual feelings. You do indeed want to have an attraction and passion toward her, but that simply should not be the sole basis for your getting married. That is based entirely too much on emotions and feelings and not enough on rational thought. When you make purely emotional decisions like that, you will tend to not see hard truths staring you in the face—hard truths like you barely know this person or, besides sex, you have absolutely nothing in common. You may only see what you want to see and turn a blind eye to everything else.

Marriage is another one of those relationships that you should not take lightly. It is not just a super boyfriend-girlfriend type of thing. It is intended to be a lifetime commitment in which you and this woman are now sharing your life dreams, passions, successes, and failures. With all of that, it only makes sense that before you make such a decision, you include your head and not just your heart.

Regarding marriage, you cannot be naive and think that love is all you need. Well, unfortunately for me but fortunately for you, I can tell you a little bit about that. Like everything in this book, it is up to you to decide what to do with it. I have a really good friend who has been married for just over thirty years, as have I. The difference between us is that he has been married to the same woman, while I am on my third wife. My present wife and I are working on our fourteenth year, and please believe me when I tell you I finally got it right.

My first wife, my son's mother whom I mentioned earlier in the book, and I simply had no business marrying each other. Not only did we not know each other, I didn't even know myself very well. I learned some really good lessons from wife number one and married wife number two. The good news is that I did not make the same mistakes with the second wife; however, wife number two taught me the hard life lesson that you definitely can't control everything that happens in your life. Wife number two came at me with a whole new bag of tricks. It became apparent that we had life plans; however, hers did not include me. I can laugh about it now, but when it was going down, there wasn't a dang thing funny about it. In fact, it was one of the hardest times in my life, but it prepared me to be the man and husband that God intended me to be in the future. *Life Lesson*: Sometimes to get you where you need to be, God will allow you to go through some tough trials and tribulations. Endure and learn the lesson, and it will make you a better person in the end.

Some of you might be thinking, *Why should I listen to this guy tell me about marriage when he has been divorced twice?* That is a very good question, and I would say to that, "Life experience." Without a doubt, there is much to learn from my friend who has been married to the same woman for thirty years, and there is also plenty to learn from a guy like me who is willing to admit my imperfections and share the hard lessons learned from my loss, pain, and failures. I have learned from my mistakes and those made by others. I have always said, "What's the use of enduring hard life lessons if I'm not willing to share and help others?" You have something I did not, and that is a book like this one to help you along the way, so there's no excuse for you not to at least think about these things in advance.

Let's talk about some things that you will need to make a marriage work. For starters, ensure that you understand that marriage is real life and not a fairy tale. It's not like you find the right woman, fall madly in love, and live happily ever after. If you are blessed to find the right person, that is just the beginning. Also, understand that there is no such thing as a perfect person—and yes, that includes you. So right from the start, stop expecting a wife to be perfect. She will make mistakes just like you will. Marriage is about two imperfect and separate individuals coming together with a mutual goal of growing as one. No longer does the selfish "it's all about me" mentality work. For a marriage to work, the two of you must put the needs of the other before yourselves. You will always need to be thinking how any and all of your actions can adversely affect your wife. It is also vital that nothing and no one come before your wife. That does include all family and friends.

Hopefully, you already see just how deep the marriage commitment is or at least should be. Just the very concept of two individuals trying to become one is pretty mind blowing. So far you spent your life trying to define who you are, and now you and another individual are to come together and grow as one heart and one mind. So how does one do that? you might ask. Well, for starters, it certainly begins with ensuring that you really know this person you are attempting to grow as one with. When I say "really know" someone, you must first understand it is going to take some time for that to happen. I can't give you a time frame, but I will tell you that it's more than a few weeks or months and in some cases years. It takes time to really see and understand who a person is. Just think about how complex and moody you can be. Why would you not think someone else would be the same way, if not more so than you?

We all have likes and dislikes of our own, as well as our good points and not-so-flattering points. Human nature, particularly between the sexes, is that we want our good points to outshine our not-so-good points by a lot. If you are truly interested in a woman, you will do everything you can to show what a good man you are and try to hide or minimize everything else. Trust me, she will be doing the same thing. With that said, it's going to take some time for those blinders to come off so you can start to get some glimpses into the real person. So when those glimpses pop through, I strongly suggest that you take notice and not ignore them.

Ignoring them is what I did early on. When people would show me signs of who they really were, instead of addressing it, I would make excuses for their actions. Instead of believing anything negative about them, I chose to believe what I wanted instead of what was staring me in the face. Believe me, if you are making excuses for a person early on, things aren't going to magically get better from there. If you are seeing things that concern you while you are in the "see the best of me" stage, what the heck is going to happen when she completely reveals who she truly is? Again, getting to know someone takes time. Marriage and fatherhood will be the biggest commitments you will make in your life. So without a doubt, it is well worth your investment of time on the front end.

Marriage vows are not just words; they are a promise you make in front of God and others. It is not just the culmination of an exciting courtship. It's serious business. Please learn from my mistakes and go into it with the mind-set that you are only doing this once, as God intended it to be.

Now let's say for the sake of argument that you have listened to me and took the time to learn about the woman you want to spend the rest of your life with. You decide she is who she proclaims to be and that her good outweighs the bad. So you get hitched (old-fashioned word for *married*). Now you live happily ever after? Not so fast, youngster—you are only just getting started. Remember, you are still two individuals with a plan to grow as one. Your journey is no longer just yours alone; it is now a mutual one and it has just begun. There is much more you will continue to learn about each other. You will learn things about this person that you had no clue about. Don't panic—this is just a part of the process of marriage. It took some time for you to become you, so it is going to take some time for you two to become one. Just like everything else in life worth having, you are going to have to work at it. Marriage is a lot of things, but easy is not one of them. But it is well worth the effort if you are blessed enough to be holding the right hand as you continue on your journey.

Some of you think you will never get married. The main reason for this sentiment is probably purely carnally based, meaning that the thought of getting married and making love to only one person for the rest of your life can scare some men to death. I think by now you know where I stand on this subject. God intended for marriage to be between one man and one woman in holy matrimony. We were not intended to be jumping around from woman to woman. I won't attempt to beat you over the head with this. However, after a lifetime of mistakes, I have learned that life is much easier and better when you live it according to His plan. Perhaps you are a lot smarter and wiser than I was. However, I have learned that nothing of true substance comes from a mind driven by sexual lust.

Marriage requires effort by the husband and the wife. While she may be your wife, she is still an individual who has to make her own decisions. She is also responsible and accountable for her actions just as you are. That is another reason to make sure you know the person you are marrying. Ensure that you both are aware of what being married means to the other and understand the work needed by both for success.

Most marriages don't start off rough because you are both so in love and the sex is intense, passionate, and consistent. So the hard work isn't required at first. However, after a while, when the "honeymoon" is over, as they say, you realize that you really are married and this person is here to stay, the challenges begin. Now you start to see some of the not-so-flattering things about your beautiful spouse. Remember, she is seeing and thinking the same about you.

Now is a good time to mention a few key elements that you are going to want to lock into your brain regarding marriage. These elements are honesty, trust, respect, compromise, and communication. These are important in any relationship as we previously descussed, but they are especially important in a relationship that is supposed to be the ultimate lifetime union. While I won't go into much more detail than we have already discussed, I will hit a few key points. Other than love, which hopefully is a given since you got married. I would say these five elements are key to a fundamentally sound foundation of a successful marriage. We have already talked about three of these elements (honesty, trust, and respect) in this chapter, but now we will focus on them in marriage.

Honesty in Marriage

Without honesty, it is only a matter of time before serious issues arise. If you aren't honest with your wife, your lies will eventually come to light. Lies, regardless of the reason, will eventually cause cracks in the foundation of your marriage. Hopefully, you remember what happens when you build a house (in this case, a marriage) on a faulty foundation. That's right—when the trouble comes, as it always does, the house has a poorer chance of being able to withstand the winds. It is important that you have complete honesty in your marriage. *Life Lesson*: Life is easier in a marriage when you don't have to try to remember your lies. A good point to remember is that if you need to lie about it, then you need to avoid it altogether.

Trust in Marriage

Trust goes right along with honesty. If you are in a marriage that is without trust, regardless of how the trust was compromised, it is a terrible place to be. If you recall, trust is one of those things that is hard earned yet easily lost.

In a marriage, the probable number-one reason for lost trust is infidelity. It's not a surprise, right? Cheating on your wife and having an intimate relationship outside your marriage is often the deal breaker in a marriage. Even if it's not, the marriage is permanently scarred, and all the hard work you put into attaining your spouse's trust can be gone in a matter of minutes. Whether you are the guilty party of causing the lost trust or the person who has lost trust in his spouse, neither is a nice place to be. If you have lost the trust, you will no longer believe your spouse is who she says she is. If you caused the lost trust, you now have to live with the negative consequences of your poor choice and bad decisions.

The thing about lost trust as a result of infidelity is that it not only hurts you, but it affects the lives of others who love you. You can give plenty of excuses for your actions, but it still comes down to your choices and decisions. You have to decide early on what type of man and husband you are going to be. Just because you get married does not mean you are blind or no longer face temptation. In fact, just know it's coming and have a plan to shut it down when it pops up. Hopefully, you got married for a lifetime commitment. Sex outside your marriage is lust, not love. Nothing good can come from cheating. Sure, you get a few minutes of superficial pleasure, but then what? Not only did you compromise your marriage, you have also compromised the character of the man you are trying to become. Jumping into bed with another woman is not hard to do; however, it will take a real man of sound character (and discipline) to deny his fleshly desires when faced with this temptation. When faced with extreme temptation, it is imperative you shut it down quickly because the longer you think about it, the greater chance it has of becoming reality.

Life Lesson: Any and all negative actions first started off as a simple thought. You can't always control things in your life, but you can control what you choose to think about—your thoughts and your actions are your responsibility. Be smart and think it out before you act. Don't forget to ask yourself, "Is it worth it?" before you do it. And don't ask simply if it is worth it if you get caught, but is it worth the damage to your character?

> *"Can a man take fire in his bosom and his clothes not be burned? Or can a man walk on hot coals and his feet not be scorched?"*
>
> *—Proverbs 6:27–28*

Respect in Marriage

For a marriage to work, you not only need to have a foundation made up of love, honesty, and trust, but you also need to have respect for your wife. Respect her not only as your life mate but as a woman and a person. Respect her enough to treat her like the queen of your kingdom. Respect her thoughts and opinions. Respect her enough not to call her something other than her name. Respect her enough to build her up and not tear her down. Respect her enough to never allow your anger and frustration to lead to verbal or physical abuse. Respect her enough to love her and care for her emotional and physical needs. If you are unable to do all of these, then perhaps you are not ready for marriage or this is not the woman for you. These are all questions you need to ask yourself before you get married. Remember, your wife is not just some random chick. Failure to show her respect is disrespectful not only to her but to you as well—and the man I hope you strive to be.

Compromise in Marriage

The next word you will need to know is *compromise*. It is defined as "a settlement of differences by natural concessions; an agreement reached by adjustment of conflicting or opposing claims." Compromise is vital to marital success. Remember the whole two-becoming-one thing? That simply does not happen without compromise. There has to be some give and take by both parties. There will be things you both feel strongly about, but your views may be opposing. This is when you will need to discuss calmly and come to some kind of agreement. Whatever you do, don't go into marriage with an attitude of "I'm the man, and what I say goes." For some women, that might work for a while, but all that will do is cause trouble down the road (this is female example number one). After time, it will turn into resentment because she will feel you do not respect her thoughts and opinions. Then there are some women for whom that won't work from day one (female example number two). This woman will require sound, reasonable discussion rather than the "because I told you so" argument.

Speaking from experience, I will tell you that the example number one woman may appear more appealing because it just seems easier and provides less drama. While it may appear easier, that ease will fade after a while when it turns into resentment, which can be a killer to a marriage. The problem with resentment in a marriage is that it usually does not reveal itself for quite some time. Whatever the issues were, they have never really been resolved—only moved out of sight for a while. By then, they have had time to fester and grow into something that could have possibly been avoided had you just really listened and compromised. *Life Lesson*: All people, not just your wife, want to be heard—not kind of heard but really heard. It is a sign that even if you don't agree, at least you have enough respect for them as people to hear them out.

Female example number two would have never let the issue grow to the point of its turning into resentment. She would have made her stance known from the start. Don't be intimidated by this approach; just learn to talk and compromise when need be. With female example number one, you can let your pride and ego get away from you. If you're not careful, you can become a bit of a dictator because it looks and feels like it has been working for so long. Then—boom! Everything blows up because she has had her fill of the one-way marriage, and resentment is now living in your house. You will probably think it just happened all of a sudden, but it didn't; it took some time to get there. You just weren't paying attention because you got stuck on only seeing things your way. Example number one is not necessarily weak, but she may be passive, preferring to avoid confrontation. However, if resentment takes hold, she will become passive-aggressive and start defying you in her own subtle ways.

Female example number two is overtly stronger, and if she doesn't think things are right, she will let you know. She will not allow the resentment to grow unless you still don't listen. I have been married to example number one, and I am presently married to a strong example number two kind of woman. It is my opinion that if you are a man of strong character, you will need the strength of an example number two female to complement your strength. This will make you a more complete man in the long run. She will challenge you to be the best man you can be.

In the area of compromise, it's not about winning or losing with your wife. It is about mutual respect and understanding. If the issue is not that big of a deal to you but it appears very important to her, then a compromise can be the key to peace in your home. Compromise is very much a two-way street. It can't always be your way, nor can it always be her way either. If you want to save yourself some headaches in the future, then take your time before you get married so you can give yourselves a chance to know more about each other.

I truly believe it is better to have a strong woman in your corner with whom compromise is needed than a passive one who will let you have your way all of the time. The strong woman will always keep it real with you, so you will know exactly what you are dealing with. The passive woman, by not telling you how she truly feels, can be a problem to your marriage because your foundation is not based on honesty. It needs to be noted that, with example number one, you need to ensure that she is comfortable telling you her concerns without you becoming aggressive. On your journey, seek to be a man of strong character and reinforce that with a wife of strength and equal character.

Communication in Marriage

We have talked about honesty, trust, respect, and compromise. The fifth key element is communication. Communication is vital. Here is a news flash to some of you—communication is not just about you verbalizing to your wife all the things that you don't like. This sounds pretty basic, I know, but I have learned that you cannot assume everybody knows that communication does indeed involve talking. However, if you want it to be effective, I strongly suggest that you learn to listen intently to what your wife is trying to tell you. I also suggest that you keep an eye out for the things not spoken. An example of this would be if your wife has been strongly voicing her opinion on a particular issue for quite some time but then you start noticing that she's no longer talking about it. Don't start patting yourself on the back because you think you finally wore her down and she has come around to seeing things your way. It could be a host of other things, including that she is thinking you don't respect her thoughts or feelings enough to even hear her out. It could also mean she realizes you are an idiot on this particular subject and has simply decided not to focus her energy on this battle. Either way, it's up to you to communicate and find out.

When I say listen to her, I don't mean to simply hear some of the words coming out of her mouth, but really listen to the passion and sentiment of what she is attempting to share with you. With us being men and them women, some of the things they talk about may sound like pure nonsense to us, but ensure that you hear her out primarily because you love her and respect what is important to her. Nothing is easy about communication. Even after all of these years, I am still working on it. One thing about me is that I may be a bit hardheaded at times, but I can't deny sound and factual reasoning. My wife may tell me something with which I initially strongly disagree, but if what she said makes sense, I can't ignore it. She knows me well enough to know that she doesn't need to nag me about something. She puts it out there, and then it's up to me to decide what I do with it. If she's right, I have to admit it. We can move on after I have a talk with myself along the lines of, "Dang, she is right again." Trust me—this type of understanding does not occur overnight, but I not only love her but also respect her enough to hear her.

I guess now would be a good time to mention that if you are wrong about something, do not be too proud to apologize to your wife. Just make sure it is sincere and that you are not saying it so much that the words "I'm sorry" stop meaning anything. Hopefully, your apology will be followed up by some type of change of attitude or action. An overly simplified example of this is if your wife is constantly asking you to help around the house and you say you will. You also apologize for not being more helpful since you both work. However, if there is no change in your actions, like actually helping more, then your apologies will start to mean nothing after a while. By the way, keeping your home tidy is not just your wife's job, particularly if you both work. Granted, she does some things better than you and vice versa, but make an effort to help her because she gets tired too. Here is some bonus advice: Make sure you let her know you appreciate the things she does for you. Don't take things for granted. Don't start to think that you are the king and your wife does what she does because she has to. She does it because she loves you and wants to make you happy. My wife retired a few years before I did, and one day I was teasing her and said, "What do you do around here all day?" She in turn said, "Whatever it is, I will stop doing it, and then you tell me what I do." Never made that little joke again.

Early on, you and your spouse will have some real failures in the communication department. Either you will just stop talking altogether, which is never a good thing, or you will have some rather warm to very heated arguments. Neither are foreign to marriage, but you don't want these arguments to be the norm either. The key elements of respect and compromise will come in handy during these times. It is very important that you both learn how to fight. I am not talking about throwing blows; I'm talking about how to communicate when emotions and tempers are high. Although you may be angry, this woman is still your wife, and you love and respect her. This is a very critical time, and I highly recommend that you think before you speak while in an agitated state (go back and reread the section on anger if need be). I also recommend early on that you and your wife discuss and set some ground rules for when disagreements arise. When you set those ground rules, please make sure to include not bringing up the word *divorce* when things are heated. You don't want to start throwing around that word just because you are angry at that moment.

It is important that you understand the power of your words. While engaged in one of those heated communication sessions, you may say something that, as soon as it rolls off your tongue, you already know you messed up. Sometimes things said just can't be unheard, and once they're said, they can't be unsaid. Accepted apologies for something stupid you may have said will vary from person to person, so I suggest you seriously think before you let certain things slip from your lips.

Regarding thinking before you speak, I read an acronym somewhere that relates to this. I can't remember where I saw it, but I wrote it in my notes because I knew it would be handy one day. The acronym is THINK: T—Is it true? H—Is it helpful? I—Is it inspiring? N—Is it necessary? and K—Is it kind? I'm sure that if we run that through our heads before we speak, it could save us a whole lot of trouble.

> *"The heart of the wise instructs his mouth and adds persuasiveness to his lips. Pleasant words are a honeycomb, sweet to the soul and healing to the bones."*
> —*Proverbs 16:23–24*

Fatherhood

Let's take some time to talk about one of the most important relationships you will ever be involved in, and that is the role of a father to your children. This is the relationship (or lack thereof) that sparked the writing of this book. I have spoken on my relationships with my biological father and stepfather. While neither were positive, I did learn valuable lessons that have compelled me to share with you. I had a choice to take the experiences I had with the father figures in my life and either continue the cycle of negative fatherhood or use them to find the positive. What also drove me in writing this book was that I knew many of you have come from the same type of circumstances as I. Just because we may not have had the examples of fathers that we had wished does not mean that we cannot choose to be the kind of fathers our children deserve.

Just as marriage is not something you should take lightly, the same is true about being a father, perhaps even more so. When things don't work between a husband and wife, they can file for divorce. The same is not, or should not, be true regarding a father and his children. No matter what happens in life, there is no divorce between a man and his children. If you choose not to step up to the plate and have an active role in the life of your child, then you have totally missed the mark in regard to this book.

Perhaps you were raised in some pretty bad surroundings. What you do with that experience is up to you. I hope and pray that you make better choices and decisions than the people from your negative environment. I also hope and pray that, regardless of what stage of life you are in, you decide now that when the time comes, you will be a real father to your children. To be a real father, you need to be a real man, and real men are made of real character. Choose for yourself what type of man and father you will be, and start working on making that a reality.

In an ideal world, we would all wait until we are married before we start to plan to have children. What normally happens is a guy and girl have sex when they are way too young, and the girl gets pregnant. Either the guy attempts to man up and help the girl with raising the baby, or he is suddenly nowhere to be found and the girl is left alone to handle "her problem." Unfortunately, the latter is all too common in our communities. All this does is continue the cycle of black males not evolving into black men and black children being deprived of fathers. I am not saying this happens all the time, but I am saying it happens far too often. Those of you reading this book, I am asking you to be the exception to the rule. Dare to be different; dare to be real men and fathers who not only take care of their children but also take an active role in their lives.

Now let's take it back a bit. Becoming a father does not happen by accident. It can absolutely be avoided. Again, it starts off by thinking about your choices and decisions. Just because you can get an erection does not mean you are emotionally ready to engage in sex. I say that if you feel you must do it, you need to use a condom—not sometimes, but all the time. Please don't take this to mean I am saying it's okay for you to engage in premarital sex. It simply means I am not naive enough to think that every one of you is going to wait until you are married to have sex. If you are going to do it, then be smart and use protection to avoid sexually transmitted diseases (STD) and unplanned pregnancies. Even if the girl says she is on the pill, use a condom since the pill is not a 100 percent guarantee, nor does it protect you from STDs.

Before I move forward, let's talk a bit more about sex and maturity. Trust me—I am not so old that I don't remember what it was like to be in my teens with my hormones raging like crazy. So when I tell you that you should wait to engage in sex, I am not saying it to be a "blocker." Like everything else in this book, I am sharing my life experiences with you. It is just a way for me to provide you with more tools to help you make well-informed decisions. When I talk to you about maturity before sex, I am not simply talking age because I know young men who are only in their late teens but are mature and wise beyond their years. I also know men my age who are foolish and extremely immature for their age. So regarding maturity and sex, I am talking about understanding that sex is more than the immediate physical contact, or at least it should be.

You need to understand that along with sex can come some rather serious responsibilities. When you are young, your body is telling you that you are ready for sex. Your buddies are giving you their knowledge-lacking advice that being a man means you have sex with as many women as possible. It can all get a little overwhelming. All of the external pressures to include raging hormones, peer pressure, and equally confused willing females make it all too easy to make the wrong decisions. Poor choices to engage in sex too soon based on these additional pressures can definitely lead to bad decision making.

Here is something real to think about regarding having sex too early. You have two immature people engaging in an act they really don't understand physically, emotionally, or mentally. So after the act, you go off and brag to your buddies about what you did and about how much of a man you think you are. This only confirms your immaturity. Real men don't share such intimate acts with others. It disrespects the female and yourself as well. Engaging in sex does not make you a man; all it means is that you are male. The character traits we talked about earlier are what define who you are, and a man of character does not kiss and tell.

Back to our scenario. That same girl (whose name you probably forgot by now) walks up to you eight months later with a big belly and tells you that she is having your baby. Now let's speed up through all the "how do you know it's mine" stuff and say it is your baby since you were the first and only guy she's ever had sex with. So now what? There you are at whatever age with no real clue regarding who you are and no real idea at all about who this girl is. All you really know is that eight months ago, you and she shared an act that will follow you for the rest of your life. Like it or not, in one month's time, another life that you helped create is coming into this world. Again I ask, what are you going to do?

I hope you are not waiting for me to tell you what to do. I told you from the beginning about being mature and responsible before you engage in sex. A responsible person will take into consideration, *If I do this, then that can happen*, and the "that" in this scenario is a baby, the consequence of your actions. Remember, I said you are responsible and accountable for your actions. Well, *responsible* and *accountable* mean that you do everything in your power to be the best father you can be.

Because of the lack of a father or any real male role model when I was a teenager, I vowed that if I ever became a father, I was going to do a much better job than the examples shown to me.

When I was thirteen years old, my mother had my baby brother, Alex. I think I mentioned that because my mother was having another child with my stepfather after all those years of nothing but trouble, I was extremely angry with her. In fact, my mind was made up that I was not going to have anything to do with this baby. However, that all changed the very moment I saw and held this little guy. It was love at first sight. I had never really been around a baby before. I immediately knew this tiny thing was totally dependent on us for everything in his life. Wow—what a huge responsibility. I wasn't the father, but I knew he needed me.

Because of the big age difference between Alex and me, I was always more of a father figure than a big brother to him. So I learned paternal skills early on. When my son was born a mere six years later, I was still very young, in the navy, and extremely intimidated by the responsibility of fatherhood. Being a father meant that my personal journey was about to take a major turn. Now, not only did my less-than-bright decisions affect my life; they would affect this person who would soon be calling me Daddy.

Becoming a husband was mind blowing, but it appeared mellow compared to being a dad. It suddenly became so glaringly obvious that life was no longer just about me. It was now all about this child. I refused to let him grow up like I had. I wanted so much more for him. Even after his mother and I went our separate ways and they moved four hours away, I always made sure my son knew that his father loved him dearly.

Since he didn't live with me full time, I learned early on the importance of quality time. Whenever he was with me, I was continually dropping knowledge on him, some of it probably sooner than he was prepared for, but I was dropping it anyway. Every time I watched the movie *Boyz in the Hood*, I would laugh at the relationship between Jason "Furious" Styles (Laurence Fishburne) and his son Tre (Cuba Gooding Jr.) because it was so much like that between my son and me. I knew it was my responsibility to prepare this black boy to be a black man in a world that didn't love him. Since I was barely on my own journey, we did a lot of learning and growing together. You will make a lot of mistakes along the way, but don't let that stop you from being the best father you can that your child needs you to be.

I am offering a personal challenge to you regardless of your age (either now or later): man up and be the fathers and men our children need you to be. If more men in our communities stepped up and acted like fathers to our children, they would have a much better chance of facing an unfair world.

Fathers, our kids need more than just food, clothing, and shelter; they need our time—time to show them love and time to teach and prepare them for the world so they, in turn, can teach their children and future generations. Love them enough to not only correct them when they go astray but praise them when they do well.

Our communities are dying because our black boys are not being taught how to be responsible black men. We need our men to raise their children and point them in the right direction. Our single mothers are doing the best they can, but they aren't men or fathers. Our communities need men to teach our boys how to be men—not just males, but real men of positive character, men who lead by example. We cannot fix history or repair yesterday's woes. However, the future, our tomorrows, start today, and it starts with you. Our very future as a people depends on our men stepping up. It's never too soon to decide what kind of man and father you are going to be. Neither is it too late to change your path if you have gone astray.

> *"Let your eyes look directly ahead and let your gaze be fixed straight in front of you. Watch the path of your feet and all your ways will be established. Do not turn to the right nor the left; turn your foot from evil."*
> —*Proverbs 4:25–27*

CHAPTER 6

EDUCATION AND KNOWLEDGE

"The proverbs of Solomon the son of David, King of Israel; to know wisdom and instruction, to discern the sayings of understanding; to receive instruction in wise behavior, righteousness, justice and equity; to give prudence to the naive, to the youth knowledge and discretion. A wise man will hear and increase in learning; and a man of understanding will acquire wise counsel: to understand a proverb and a figure, the words of the wise and their riddles. The fear of the LORD is the beginning of knowledge: fools despise wisdom and instruction."

—Proverbs 1:1–7

As you read in the heading of this chapter, we will be discussing the importance of education and knowledge.

So far in this book, you have repeatedly seen some common themes, like making good choices, ensuring you think before you act, and controlling the things that you can, to name a few. Before we are done, you will see them again, along with a few more. Like a teacher once said in a class I was in, "If I tend to say things more than once, you may want to take notes because it must be important and it may be on a test somewhere down the road." So I repeat some things often for a reason, and the "test" in this situation is life. When a life test is given, it will be a surprise, closed-book exam. You will not have time to review your notes. So I suggest that you study for the test now by paying close attention to the things we talk about in this book.

Keeping with the theme of repeated statements, let's add another one: "Knowledge is power." I didn't create that one, but I do strongly believe in it. However, for it to take its full effect, lets add, "Applied knowledge is power." Without the application of the knowledge you possess, it really doesn't serve much of a purpose. It's like knowing the right thing to do but never doing it.

> *"Apply your heart to discipline and your ears to words of knowledge."*
> —*Proverbs 23:12*

The Importance of Education

Too often in our communities, our young men do not take advantage of even basic education. Now, I understand that not all educational opportunities are fair and equal across our nation. However, with that said, it is even more important to take full advantage of the educational opportunities that are available.

Compared to most of the world, the United States is still in its infancy. Not that long ago, it was against the law for slaves to read or to be taught to read. Our ancestors were beaten and some killed because they dared to seek basic knowledge. Why do you think there was such a law in the first place? I am sure there are many related reasons, but it would be a safe bet to say it had a lot to do with it being much easier to control people if they were kept blinded by the darkness of ignorance. Slave masters knew that if they prevented slaves from attaining education, they could limit them to only the things that benefited them, the slave owners. They knew that if they controlled the slave's knowledge, they could keep their world small and isolated to the will of the slave masters. Our people were beaten and killed because of their thirst for knowledge. What could we possibly give as an acceptable excuse for not seeking it today?

Entirely too many of our young people simply feel that school has nothing to offer them. They couldn't be more wrong. Trust me when I tell you that negative consequences follow the poor decision to leave school or not seek further education. We have already established that things aren't fair or easy. So knowing that and removing it as an excuse, what reason do we use for not seeking knowledge now?

Education is often treated as an option, and I guess it is since you can choose not to go to school. Or you can go to school but choose not to learn. Please make sure you understand that by being a man of color, the deck has already been stacked against you. Why make it harder than it has to be? That's exactly what you do when you go out on your journey without education. Life is hard enough on its own without you making it harder.

Again, while you cannot control all things in your life, ensure that you control the things you can. Your education is one of those things that you do have some say in. Seek education and knowledge as if your quality of life is dependent upon it. While life may never be fair and equal for people of color, you can at least raise the bar by seeking all the knowledge you possibly can.

Life will give you things, and it will also take things away from you. The thing about education and knowledge is that once you get it, it cannot ever be taken away from you. That is why applied knowledge is power. Once your mind has been opened, your horizons expand. The world is now much bigger than just your neighborhood or your city. Once your eyes and mind are opened, your self-perceived limitations no longer seem as oppressive. However, without knowledge, your vision is narrowed and it is difficult to see past the walls directly in front of you.

Knowledge allows you to think and see that there has to be more to life than the boundaries immediately in front of you. Knowledge allows you to think about how your life can be if you go around, over, under, or even through whatever the barrier may be. Lack of education can stifle your ability to dream because it hinders your ability to even think further than your present situation. Education and the gathering of knowledge will enable you to make better choices and decisions. Instead of making your choices based on impulse or what may feel good right now, knowledge will allow you to think and ask yourself, *Is this the best thing for me to do?*

In the Bible, there is a story about Samson and Delilah. Samson was an extraordinarily physically strong man. His enemies could not defeat him no matter what they tried. So his enemies got the idea to use Samson's female friend, Delilah, against him, and she went along with it. (This was the second time Samson's enemies tried this trick.) Delilah kept on nagging Samson until he finally gave in and told her the secret source of his strength. (Spoiler: It was his hair.)

Once they cut off his hair, he was just a normal guy. He was captured and literally blinded to make sure he was in their control. That was an extremely short version of the story. What I want you to get out of it is that by not seeking education and knowledge, you are giving up your power and vision just as Samson did. The difference is that the source of your power is no secret to your enemy, which is anything or anybody that holds you back, including yourself. Your enemy already knows that your power is minimized if you allow him to blind you to the importance of attaining education.

> *"The mind of the prudent acquires knowledge, and the ear of the wise seeks knowledge."*
> —*Proverbs 18:15*

Being Proactive versus Reactive

I am sure that when I started on the subject of education, you probably thought that I was going to talk about the importance of going to college. Well, if that's what you thought, then you were correct. However, before you get to college, you need to get through middle and high school first.

One of the things I hope to accomplish in this book is to get you to be more proactive in your life than just reactive. When you are more focused on just dealing with things in life as they come your way (reactive), you spend all your time and energy being on the defense. In football terms, you rarely score points on the defensive side of the ball. In life, as in football, you need an offensive plan of attack if you want to score points. Being proactive in your life is like being on offense in football with you playing quarterback. To score points, you need to come up with a plan (plays in football). Not only do you need a plan, but you must put the plan in action (run the plays). A plan or playbook is useless if you don't activate it in life or on the field. If your defensive players stay on the field for most of the game, chances are they are going to get tired. When the defense is tired, the other team's offense can score at will. It is always better to be the one scoring the points.

Also, in football, since you don't have the ball while you are on defense (not in control), it is your job to react to what the offense is throwing your way (being reactive in life). However, when you are on offense (being proactive in life), you have an opportunity to dictate the outcome of the game. Sometimes plays and life plans don't work, but you don't quit the game. You refocus the plan of attack, get back out there, and try again. Be proactive about what goes into the planning and the execution of your plans.

This whole football metaphor is just to help you to understand that, in life, it is always better to be proactive rather than simply reactive. Education is going to require you to be not only proactive in the creation of your action plan but also interactive (involved) in the execution of that plan. The sooner you start to create and activate that plan, the better. So if you are presently in grade, middle, or high school or even out of school, get yourself a plan of action for the pursuit of as much education as possible. There is no such thing as having too much education or knowledge. The more education you have, the greater of a chance you have of achieving the positive goals you set for yourself.

Setting Goals

I just mentioned having an action plan or plan of attack. Setting goals will come in extremely handy in the formation of your life plan (goals). The following are a few things that you will need in setting goals. First, set your goal or identify what it is you wish to attain or accomplish. For example, let's make going to and finishing college your goal. Second, have a plan for attaining your goal. Part of the planning for this goal needs to include things you can control, like making the best grades to qualify you for college. Also, in this stage you need start looking into grants, scholarships, and overall funding of this goal. Third, ensure that your goal and planning is realistic. If your goal is to attend Yale or Harvard but all you get on your report cards are C's, this goal may not be realistic. You are going to have to either seriously up your grades or choose other colleges. Also, include some target dates to accomplish your goals. That will help you stay focused and accountable for attaining your goals. Fourth, write your goals down and review them frequently. Also, write notes regarding your proactivity in achieving your goals. If you have a written goal of attending college but are cutting class every week, you are not being proactive or interactive in attaining the goals you set for yourself. In fact, all you have is some stuff you wrote down on paper. Fifth, establish your priorities in attaining your goals and focus intently on them. If you say getting good grades is a priority, but instead of doing your assignments and studying you are partying every night, obviously your focus is not on your identified priority. Instead, focus on your goal and avoid anything that may distract or hinder you from attaining your goal.

These are just a few things I have always included in setting and pursuing my goals. This particular example I used was education because it is the subject at hand; however, the same format can be used in the establishment of any goal. On a related side note, we are complex,beings so as you review your goals remember that you are constantly evolving. With that said, make not only short-term goals but long-term ones as well. How you think today will not or at least *should* not be how you think down the road. Let goals evolve but not disappear altogether. If you set the bar too low, the only person you cheat is yourself.

In the setting of goals, it is important to remember that life doesn't always go according to our plans, but that is still no excuse for not having goals and plans. Do not hesitate to seek the help of others in the planning of your goals. Part of knowledge is acknowledging what you don't know. You don't have to know everything, but know where to seek help. Don't ever forget that just because you don't immediately succeed at something does not mean you are a failure. You only fail when you quit trying.

I have set numerous goals in my life, but I would like to share one in particular with you as an example of setting a goal and going after it. When I was still a correctional officer at the prison, I once saw this group of special agents from the Special Service Unit (SSU) come to the institution for a very high-profile investigation. I immediately knew that I wanted to become an SSU special agent because of the way these men carried themselves and the respect they were given. When I asked what I needed to do to be one of them, I was told I would have to be at the level of a captain, which was three levels higher than my present position. At that moment, I knew I needed to start earning promotions if I was ever going to have a shot at being an SSU special agent. At the time, I had no idea that there were no more than twenty-five SSU special agents in the whole state. So being black and getting into SSU was going to be a major challenge, to say the least.

Soon after that initial encounter, I set my goal to be an SSU special agent. My immediate plan was to first be promoted to sergeant and then eventually lieutenant. At the time, I had no idea if my plan was realistic, but I knew that if I didn't earn those promotions, it would definitely never happen. My thought process was that I might not reach my goal, but it was not going to be because I didn't try. I wrote my goals and priorities down and reviewed them often.

I put my plan into action. I had to make some adjustments along the way, but after about ten years, I eventually made it to the streets as an SSU special agent. After another ten years of being a special agent and a senior special agent, I retired as head of the CDC's entire street law enforcement unit. All of that started off as a simple thought of me daring to think I could be a special agent. Now, please don't think I made it happen because I'm all that, because I am not. It took several people seeing something in me and giving me a chance, and most importantly God directing my path. In actuality, by going for my goal, far more things were outside my control than within it. I could only control the things I could and let everything else take care of itself. If it were meant to be, it would happen. If I didn't do my part, my goal would have been just all talk and no action.

> *"Without consultation, plans are frustrated, but with many counselors they succeed."*
> —*Proverbs 15:22*

In Pursuit of Knowledge

I understand that attending college just may not be for you, but I don't want you to discard the idea totally without at least thinking about it. I know I have mentioned a few times about life not being fair particularly for men of color. It is your choice to either use that as an excuse not to try or get proactive in your life and use it to motivate you. I am a firm believer that seeking higher education is certainly a way to be proactive in your future. While it may not make things completely fair, it will open more doors of opportunity to you. It's up to you to walk through those doors once they have been opened.

Higher education not only opens your minds and feeds your intellect, a college degree shows the world and future employers that you are capable of setting, pursuing, and attaining a goal. A college degree reinforces that you are indeed capable of starting and finishing something. If you choose not to pursue college, it does not mean you cannot find success in life, but it can make your journey harder.

Most of the advice in this book is from my personal experiences. Unfortunately for me (again, fortunately for you), some of these experiences came from some bad choices and decisions I made earlier in my journey. When I say *unfortunately*, I don't mean it in a negative manner. I mean it to say that it was unfortunate for me that it took some bad decisions and learning some hard lessons to get me to the place I am today. However, those experiences are what prepared me to be able to share these lessons with you. So for me it has all been worth it if at least one person receives something from this book to help them on their journey.

Early on in this book, we talked about some of my high school years and the fact that I barely graduated. The sad thing about me and high school is that it never had anything to do with it being too hard for me. (Well, maybe math. That always did kick my butt.) In fact, I have always really enjoyed learning new things. Even to this today, I love things that make me say, "Wow, I didn't know that." I will always have a thirst for knowledge. I have always said that the day you stop learning is the day you stop living. The thing about education and knowledge is that the more you know, the more you know what you don't know. Never stop learning.

I remember in my middle school days there was a bookmobile (a mini library on wheels) that would come to the neighborhood. I would ditch my friends so I could find some books to check out. I thought cool kids didn't hang out at a library, even if it was on wheels. I knew when I opened a book that it was a way to escape my present surroundings, to open my mind to the possibility that there was so much more out there than our little neighborhood.

I think my passion for reading comes from my third-, fourth-, and fifth-grade teachers, Mrs. O'Neal and Mr. West. They had a unique way of teaching. Every day after lunch they would read books to the class. I remember letting my imagination go wherever the stories took me. They opened not only our minds but also our eyes by taking us on amazing field trips to museums, the ocean, and even a camping trip to Yosemite National Park. I will forever be indebted to those two teachers for the seeds of knowledge they planted in me. They have no idea of the foundation they laid for me over forty years ago. It may have taken awhile, but by the grace of God those seeds did indeed finally flourish. That is what I'm attempting to do in you—plant seeds of wisdom in your heart and mind. Just like it was with me, it will be up to you what you do with them. A special round of applause goes out to America's unsung heroes, our teachers.

When I started thinking I was the two C's (too cool and too cute) in high school, I got seriously sidetracked and focused on everything but my education. I did only enough to get by and often not even that. If I did show up to class, I barely paid attention. Knowing me, I paid more attention to the cute girls than to the teachers.

As I look back, I still shake my head at all the effort I put into wasting my God-given potential. Like Coach Washington, the football coach, once told me, "There is much more to life than being cool." I truly want to stress those same words to you now. Education is so much more important than being cool and popular. All of those things may seem important when you are young and foolish. However, unlike education and knowledge, they will fade away. That is why I can't stress enough the importance of not only building your body but your mind as well. The only way your attained knowledge won't fade away is if you choose to apply it to your life.

I had to learn these things the hard way; hopefully, you won't do the same. I have said that my mistakes in life are now a major source of my present character. There have been many times when I thought that if I could go back in time to my high school days knowing what I know now, I would be the squarest, nerdiest dude in school. I'm talking black-rimmed glasses and pocket protector kind of square. I would have made Urkel from the old television show *Family Matters* look cool. My nose would have stayed in the books. There would have been no time for partying and fast girls. I now know that absolutely nothing should ever be more important than your education. Education requires long-term dedication in preparing for the future. I now know that I was young, dumb, and extremely short-sighted. I couldn't see past the right now. *Long-term* to me back then meant the party that was coming up on Saturday.

You remember when I talked about being proactive instead of just reactive when it comes to your life? To do that requires vision and planning. I now know the kids I went to school with who became doctors and lawyers had plans, and they put them into action starting way back then. They didn't wait until they were in their twenties to suddenly decide they wanted to be doctors or lawyers. Being proactive takes planning, focus, and discipline in the pursuit of your dreams. When you think no one in the world believes in you, then you have to believe in yourself. If people tell you that you can't do something, then they are fools; and if you believe them, you are foolish as well. If I didn't believe in you, I wouldn't be spending all this time writing this book for a bunch of foolish people. So for those people who tell you that you will never amount to anything, don't say anything; just show them how wrong they are.

> *"Every prudent man acts with knowledge, but a fool displays folly."*
>
> —*Proverbs 13:16*

I never attended a four-year college. However, before going to the navy, I did take several fire science courses at my local community college. I thought I was going to be a firefighter, but I didn't finish and went to the navy on my nineteenth birthday. Several years later, long after getting out of the navy and working in the prison, I started to take classes again at the community college. Work, family, and life got in the way, but after many years, I finally got my associate of arts degree in public safety. By the time I received it, it did nothing to help my career since by then I was already a special agent. However, it was important to me because it was a personal challenge to myself to finish what I had started. Again, by the grace of God, things worked out for me, but there is a much easier route than the one I chose. Pay attention, young men, and make your education one of your highest priorities, if not *the* highest.

In the last chapter ("Relationships"), we talked about friends and the importance of choosing wisely the people you hang out with. When it comes to your education, it is very important that you hang with other like-minded, education- and goal-oriented individuals—people who encourage education, not laugh at it. My godson is in his final year at the University of California–Davis. He recently told me that while he was in high school, he was one of the smartest kids. However, once he hit the college campus, he was immediately humbled by the sheer brilliance of some of his peers. He said that most of the kids in his immediate social group were smarter than him. However, that does not deter him in the slightest because he knows that he can and will simply have to outwork them. That's exactly the attitude I want you to have. When things get tough in school and life, it simply means you have to work harder.

I do understand that not everyone has a desire or the ability to go to college. Fortunately, knowledge is not only gained in college. However, it must be sought out by expanding your mind through the reading of quality materials with real educational value. Even when my silly butt didn't go to school as I should have, I still enjoyed learning things through the pages of a book.

I am a firm believer that you should always be in the midst of a book with your next book all ready to go. You may have a hard time believing this, but if you turn off the television and pick up a book, you will not get sick from television withdrawal. There is so much knowledge out there just waiting for you to seek it out.

One thing about today's technology is that you can have your entire library on your tablet or even on your phone. I am not one to adapt to change easily, but one of the best gifts I ever received was a Kindle Fire tablet for Christmas a few years ago. It took me a little time to get used to it, but once I did it was all about constantly searching for my next book. I have certainly come a long way from my navy days, when I would be out at sea for months and going through books like they were going out of style. There were no tablets back then, so I had to do it the old-fashioned way and pay a visit to the ship's library.

I have always loved fiction because of its ability to take me on a journey in my mind. I also greatly enjoy nonfiction for its pure educational value. Some days I would be reading Alice Walker or Toni Morrison, and the next I would totally shift directions and read James Baldwin.

One thing about seeking knowledge via books is that it gives you an opportunity to think and see things from another's point of view. While you may not completely agree with the writer, it will at least make you think. That is the power of reading—hopefully, to make you a thinker rather than a mindless follower with no ideas or thoughts of your own.

As I said before, we should always be in a state of growing and evolving into the men we desire to be. The seeking of knowledge, specifically through books, greatly contributes to your growth. Once you acknowledge that you don't know everything and our world is truly a big place filled with so much to learn, then you can understand what it means to have your mind open and not just your eyes. Failure to seek education and knowledge not only hurts you but can also be hurtful to your offspring in the future. If you are without education or knowledge, it is virtually impossible to share either with your children.

I will never forget that when my sister and I were young, there were a couple of occasions when my stepfather would give us his mail and say something like, "Read this so I can see how smart you are." We didn't realize it then, but Mom finally told us that he could not read. I found out that when he was in high school, he had been a very talented baseball player. Because of his skill on the baseball field, he was able to graduate from high school without the ability to read.

So all of you athletes out there, being a great athlete is well and good, but never forget that sports lasts for a season, while knowledge lasts for a lifetime. Invest in your mind and not just your athletic ability. I guarantee that the day will come when you can no longer play sports, and it is your responsibility to ensure that you are prepared for that day. It hurts my heart when I hear stories of amazing athletes who made millions of dollars during their sports careers but ended up with absolutely nothing at the end of their careers. Then they have no money, and some have no real education or transferable skills to make a living. That's not even including all the amazing athletes in college who never made it to the professional level. They spent years in college playing sports but not preparing themselves for the possibility of not making it to the pros. Of course, that is not all athletes, but unfortunately it is the truth for far too many. Suddenly, they find themselves at the "Now what?" point. Young men, if you find yourselves blessed to be able to attend college while you play sports, please take advantage of the educational opportunities you have been presented.

Have a Plan B and a Plan C in the event that your dream of playing pro sports does not happen.

Just another point to reinforce the importance of being proactive in your future—life is hard enough without compounding it by going on your journey without every tool possible. One of the most important tools you can ever have is education and knowledge. On your life journey, it is important that you plan ahead. Life is like playing chess, not checkers. You must think several moves ahead.

In life, you will encounter potholes, pitfalls, roadblocks, and mountains on the path of your journey. Education and knowledge will help you to recognize and navigate around obstacles. Without education and knowledge, you may miss the warning signs and attempt to go through or over the mountain when you don't have to. Sure, you may be successful and get to the other side, but you made it much harder than it needed to be.

> *"By wisdom, a house is built, and by understanding it is established, and by knowledge, the rooms are filled with precious and pleasant riches."*
> *—Proverbs 24:3–4*

CHAPTER 7

EMPLOYMENT AND FINANCES

I n the last chapter, we talked about the importance of education. In this chapter, we will talk about putting education and knowledge to work in the employment world. We will also talk a little about finances later in the chapter.

I officially joined the workforce when I was fourteen years old and in the ninth grade. I say *officially* because when I was around ten years old, I had a newspaper route for the *Stockton News*. I delivered the paper once a week to every house in my area. The problem with the job was that the customers didn't have to pay; payment was voluntary. Once a month, I would have to go to every house that I delivered to and ask the folks if they wanted to "donate" toward the paper they never asked for. I lived on the south side of town, and these people, like my mother, didn't have extra money to donate. A few folks would feel sorry for me and give a little something, but most either didn't open the door or just told me no.

After a while, this whole work-and-ask-for-donations thing didn't make much sense to me. So the next time I received my papers, as I was folding them, I decided I wasn't going to do it anymore, and I dumped all of them in a Dumpster. The next day, the route manager knocked at our door, and I heard her snitching me out to my mom. I didn't feel like getting a whooping, so I bolted out the back door and took off. This little runaway attempt didn't last long since I didn't have on any shoes. After a few hours, I got cold and hungry, so I returned home looking like a lost puppy. Mom hadn't even come looking for me, nor had she called the police because she knew I would be coming back soon. When she opened the door, all she said was, "Are you ready?" I said, "Yes," and I got the whopping I had coming for ditching the papers and my weak attempt at running away.

I learned two very valuable lessons that day. After the whooping, Mom told me I should have let her know that I was unhappy with the paper route. I found out that I didn't get punished for ditching the papers; I got my butt whooped because I didn't do what I had said I would do. No one made me take that job, but once I did, my mother expected me to do it like I said I would. That was one of my first real lessons in responsibility. I also learned that running away from home only worked for white kids on television because my mom wasn't coming to look for me.

I maintained my first official job (sometimes barely) with KFC until after graduating from high school. Then I went into the navy. I did just about four years in the navy, and from there I went to CDC, where I worked for the next twenty-eight-plus years. I did work at a steel warehouse for a few months while my CDC paperwork was being processed. So, officially, I have worked for four employers in my life up to this point. It's not really that many jobs, but I gained a lot of knowledge in that time.

I learned early on that, in order to not end up in prison like my father, I was going to need a job. The alternative would have been crime, selling drugs, or committing robberies and burglaries. I already knew where that lifestyle would lead me. I also knew, like Mom would always say, "All money is not good money." Sure, I could make fast money and a lot more than what I was making at KFC by being a thug, but in the end, it could and most likely would have cost me my freedom.

Anything for which the possible consequence was getting locked up was not the right decision for me. You get to make choices for yourself, so please be smart about your final decisions. If you choose the thug life, chances are you are going to have plenty of time to reflect on your bad choices. If you are one of those guys who thinks he is too good to accept a lower-paying job until he can do better, I wish you the best of luck with that. However, before you make that decision to be a thug, please take a moment to ask yourself, "Exactly how much money is my freedom worth?"

Job versus Career

How would you define the difference between having a job and having a career? I am sure the answers vary, but to me a job is usually short-term and is kept to simply pay the bills. A career is long-term with higher pay, making it harder to acquire and hopefully more rewarding. *Career* is defined as "a profession or occupation which one trains for and pursues as a lifework." That definition should lead you to see that obtaining a career is going to require you to utilize some of the things we talked about in the last chapter, including an education, planning, setting goals, and being proactive.

I am not going to attempt to tell you what type of career you should pursue, but I will tell you that the sooner you identify what your life work will be, the sooner you can start to map out your plan. When choosing a career path, pick something that will be rewarding to you, something that excites you to go to work. Since you will be spending a large part of your life in this career, it would be beneficial to you to get some enjoyment out of your chosen field.

I will also tell you that there is much more to life than just making money. Again, I am not saying that making money is bad, but don't make that your sole reason for choosing a career. Life is a lot less stressful when you enjoy what you do for a living. For example, being a doctor won't be satisfying if you do it just so you can make a lot of money. Instead, do it because you truly want to contribute to the health and well-being of others. Regardless of what career path you choose, do so as early as possible so you can determine how much education and training you will need and what type of plans and goals you will need to establish. Then be proactive in the attainment of your career goal.

When you begin to choose a career, start with identifying things you like and don't like. Be realistic—if you don't like the sight of needles or blood, then the medical field may not be the right choice for you. If you find you have a talent for debating your point, perhaps you should look into being an attorney. The career choices are numerous. It's up to you to make the choice, create a plan, and put it into action.

I started off at KFC as a cook and was an assistant manager by the time I left for the navy. While it started off as a job, it easily could have turned into a career in management. Although I was only eighteen when I left KFC, the franchise I worked for had bigger plans for me. I have to admit that the type of money they were talking about was very tempting, but something inside of me said this was not what I had planned for myself in the long haul. Everyone has to choose what's best for them. At that time in my life, I wanted to be a firefighter. In the long run, my choice to go to the navy and the CDC really worked out for me. However, in the same regard, things worked out exceptionally well for my sister who stayed with KFC and went on to do amazing things at a national level. She certainly made a lot more money than I did.

I want to make sure you understand that just as college is not for everyone, a planned career is not in the cards for everyone. Sometimes, something that starts off as a job turns out to be your life's work, and there is absolutely nothing wrong with it. Sometimes, your career chooses you, just like it did my sister. Trust me when I say I understand that sometimes a man simply has to do what he has to do. I would rather see a man washing dishes than being in jail anytime. However, if you have a choice, choose and plan a career. Choose to be proactive instead of just reactive.

> *"The hand of the diligent will rule, but the slack hand will be put to forced labor."*
>
> —*Proverbs 12:24*

Working at an Early Age

Some of you are already working or will be soon. Depending on how you look at it, working at a young age has its advantages and disadvantages. The primary disadvantage would be that if you are in school, working could take away from your studies. I would love to be able to say that was the reason I didn't get good grades in high school, but that would be a boldfaced lie. I didn't get good grades in school for primarily two reasons; first, my attendance record was terrible, and second, I simply didn't apply myself.

I am of the opinion that starting to work at an early age can have more advantages than disadvantages. It depends on your individual situation. For those of you who are like I was, I worked out of necessity. I wanted and needed things; therefore, my options were to work or thug my way through life. The latter was not a real option for me because you know how I feel about the negative consequences of the thug life.

When I was coming up as a teenager, people had to be fifteen to get a work permit to work in an established business. When I went to interview for the KFC cook job, I was only fourteen years old. I didn't attempt to lie about my age, but for whatever reason the manager saw something in me or they were extremely desperate (I'm going with the first one). Either way, I got hired on the spot without a work permit as long as my mom gave her permission, which she did. I was on my way to being a real working person. I didn't know it at the time, but the foundation of my work ethic was being laid. It guided me throughout my entire employment career.

I worked at KFC for the next four and a half years. During that time, I learned the importance of being responsible and dependable. I learned that my actions not only affected me but others as well. If I decided at the last minute that I wasn't going to show up for work, there would be a domino effect. Other employees had to be held over to cook or someone else had to come in from home on his or her day off. I learned that when I didn't show up, there was a real possibility that I could be fired. I learned to be self-reliant and independent (like when mom took my car, I had to learn which buses I needed to take to get to and from work).

Making money of my own was just one less thing my mother had to worry about. I knew other kids around my age who worked, and some of their mothers would take most of their money for various reasons, but my mom never took my money. However, it made me feel grown up to be able to offer it to her when she needed it. When I was around sixteen years old, I opened a savings account at the bank across the street from my job. One day, Mom asked me how much I had saved, and I told her I had saved just over a thousand dollars. She was blown away that I had been able to save that much money at that age. Perhaps that does not sound like a lot of money to you, but to a sixteen-year-old, south-side kid in the seventies, that was big bucks.

Since I was paying for my own stuff, I learned to really appreciate what I had. Funny how that works—when you spend your own money on something, you tend to appreciate it much more. I also learned that sometimes working meant you did things you didn't like. Cooking for KFC was far from a glamorous job. As a cook, I stayed dirty with grease and flour. And of course, I smelled like chicken all the time. For the record, it's real hard trying to talk to the girls when you smell like chicken. An advantage of working was that I had a lot less idle time, which meant a lot less time for me to get in trouble.

One of the biggest advantages for me was that working at KFC gave me real work experience, something to put on an application. Before you laugh, think about this as if you were a boss looking to hire someone. Who would you hire first—the twenty-two-year-old with a blank resume, or the twenty-two-year-old with four years of actual work experience at KFC or anywhere? Real work experience wins more times than not. In fact, I have friends who have kids who have recently graduated from four-year colleges, and they are having the hardest time finding jobs. While they have the formal education, they are lacking real-world work experience that today's employers are looking for. That tells me that the route to go is formal education combined with some real-world experience.

Setting Some Ground Rules for the Work World

I am going to give you a good mixture of items to store in your mind that will be useful to you in the work world. There's no way I can cover everything, but I am going to share some helpful insights that I have gathered along the way—things I learned from being a cook at KFC all the way to being a chief of OCS. Let's set some ground rules as we proceed.

First, I know I have said this before and, yes, I am saying it again: No one owes you anything. Nothing turns off a potential employer more than the guy who is looking for a job but comes in with a funky attitude. Remember, you are the one who is seeking a job. It truly does start with attitude. I know for a fact that if you come to me with a negative attitude, acting like you have something coming, I will be turned off immediately. The next ground rule is that if you don't have a job, then your job is looking for a job. You may not be immediately successful, but the last thing you should do is quit. We established this early on, but it deserves repeating. You are not a failure until you stop trying. If you get knocked down, get up and get back out there. Also, when you don't have a job, you need to get over your pride and humble yourself. If you are without a job, now is not the time to think you are too good or above a certain kind of job. I am not saying you have to stay there forever, but even washing dishes or cooking chicken is better than nothing until you can get on your feet.

I can't tell you how many times I have seen brothers in prison who made big money in the drug game when they were on the streets. However, when they got caught and locked up, all the people in their crew were gone. Nobody was sending them money to put on their books. Just to get things like soap and deodorant, most of these guys were doing jobs in prison that they thought they were too good to do out on the streets.

Some jobs in prison come with what is called a pay number. A pay number job will allow inmates to work and make a little money to buy things in the canteen (prison store). When I say "a little money," I mean real little. Most of the pay numbers are paid in cents per hour, not dollars. Any job on the streets is better than the best-paying job in prison.

The last ground rule for now is your attitude again. It is very important that you have a positive attitude to get and keep a job. Much earlier in the book, I mentioned that the world doesn't love you. That also means that if you have a job to do, do it. The world, specifically talking about your workplace now, doesn't care that you are having a bad day, month, or year. It doesn't care that you and your girl just broke up, nor does it care that you may have had a hard life. They care that you are going to do the job that they are paying you to do. All the other stuff is up to you to deal with and not bring to the workplace. I know that sounds harsh, but it is a reality. So chances are that if you apply for a job with a negative attitude, you are not going to get it. If you by chance get the job but your attitude sucks, there is a strong probability that you are not going to keep the job long. So a word to the wise: leave your negative attitude at home.

> *"Laziness casts into a deep sleep, and an idle man will suffer hunger."*
>
> —*Proverbs 19:15*

Getting a Job

Let's say you set your sights on a job that you feel you are qualified to do. The first thing you are going to need to do is to submit an application.

Nowadays you often do that online, so if you don't know your way around a computer, now would be the time to start learning. In the event you need to submit an application the old-fashioned way (on paper and in person), make sure to fill out the application neatly and professionally. This piece of paper represents you and is your initial introduction to the person doing the hiring. Take your time to do it right. Also, whatever you do, be factual and never lie as it will always come back and bite you in the butt. Through the years, I have been on many hiring boards, looking to hire cooks and counter people in KFC and higher management positions in CDC. So take it from me: your first introduction to the bosses most of the time is going to be your application. If it is sloppy and looks like you spent two minutes on it, your application will get put at the bottom of the stack. That would tell me, as a potential employer, that you didn't even care enough to fill out the application properly, so why should I waste my time interviewing you? If it is at all possible, which I know is difficult in today's automated world, submit the application in person so that the boss can associate a face with the application. In the event you're not hired initially, it doesn't hurt to go back a few times and resubmit an application. That shows persistence and determination, both good qualities to have in the work world.

Now let's say that your application is accepted and they want to schedule you for an interview. For starters, if you gave them your cell phone number and they call you, remember that you may not recognize the number, act like you have some sense, and don't answer the phone like is your homeboy. A simple "hello" will do.

Before the interview, you will need to do a few of things so you will be ready. First, regardless of what the job is, know a little something about the place you are applying to work. They will be impressed that you took the time to do your homework rather than just showing up. Next, remember that you are in competition with other applicants and you want to stand out in a positive manner. Do what you can to be as prepared as you can for the potential questions they may ask you. If by chance you know someone who already works there, reach out to them and pick their brain. Always have a prepared answer for the two following questions: first, "Why should I hire you over the other applicants?" and second, "Is there something else you would like to tell me about yourself before we conclude?" Both questions are your opportunity to tell the person how hard working, dedicated, loyal, and dependable you are. In other words, this is your chance to sell them on your positive attributes. Just make sure you are who you say you are.

When interview day comes, please make sure you are properly dressed and on time. Remember, you are trying to impress this potential employer. Ensure that you know exactly where you are supposed to be for the interview. Sometimes that means mapping out the interview location the day before. On the day of the interview, make sure you arrive around thirty minutes early. Arriving one minute before the interview shows a lack of desire and the inability to be prepared. Arriving early also gives you time to relax before the interview. The last thing you want is to be overly nervous when the questions begin.

When I conducted hiring interviews, I always looked for the following:

- Appearance—Did the interviewee look like he was trying to make a good impression? I always looked to see if he answered the questions with confidence and looked me in the eyes when he spoke. Looking me in the eye demonstrated confidence. Also, for most people, it is hard to lie when they are looking someone directly in the eyes.
- Clarity of speech—Ensure that you speak clearly and sound like you know what you are talking about. Use proper vocabulary; this is not the time to use street slang and a bunch of "you know what I mean?" phrases. There is no substitute for education and the ability to communicate your thoughts properly.
- Body language—Did the person's body language support the image he was trying to present? Your body language says a lot about you before you even open your mouth, including things like how you walk into the room (with confidence) and how you sit (slouched or upright). Are you overly nervous and constantly fidgeting? If you are trying to show confidence but your body language is showing something totally different, it would make me wonder what the conflict is between your words and your body language.
- Knowledge—Last, is the person knowledgeable about the job for which he is interviewing?

Depending on the job I was interviewing people for, I would look for different things. However, I considered the four areas I just mentioned every time. I always paid close attention to these things and utilized them to give me a little insight into a person's character. I know some of these sound pretty tough, but you have to remember that I spent my career as an investigator—reading people was critical in my field. Most interviewers probably won't be as tough, but it never hurts to prepare just in case they are.

Keeping the Job

Congratulations! You did an excellent job in the interview and got the call that you were selected. Now let's talk about a few all-important steps to help you keep the job, which is the goal, I hope. I have known plenty of people who are always moving from job to job. It's one thing to move from one job to another for upward mobility, but it's another thing altogether if you are moving to another job because you keep getting fired or quitting. The not-so-funny thing about these people is that no matter where they work, they believe the problem is always someone else's fault. While on occasion that may be true for you, it often means it's time for you to take a hard look at yourself if you are constantly ending up in the same situations. Be responsible and accountable for your own actions. I know I continue to talk about these self-evaluations, but trust me—it's always better to check yourself than to have others do it.

There will be times in the work world when things will happen that are totally out of your control, such as businesses closing or downsizing, requiring people to be laid off. These are things you can't do anything about. However, I am going to share some things that you can control and that will help establish a solid foundation for you in the workplace. These things must be a part of your work character. If you make them a part of who you are, then you won't need to adjust for a specific type of job. It all starts with your mentality, outlook, or attitude. I don't really care what you call it as long as you understand that, like most things in life, it all starts with the way you think.

Self-Expectations

Define from the start what you expect from yourself. Regardless of what the job may be, never set your self-expectations low. I don't care if you are a janitor or an executive, establish high expectations for yourself and always give your very best. It's about your character, and you don't want to do anything that is going to compromise it. Your character is who you are. Be the type of man you want the world to see. Don't be defined by the type of job you have or by how much money you make. Money can buy you stuff, but it cannot purchase character. No matter what the job is, you go in there with the mind-set that you are going to be the best at it.

This mind-set can and will get difficult at times when people try to get in your way because your work ethic is better than theirs or simply because they don't like you. A man of frail character will use these things as an excuse not to give his best. Let's call this the "why should I give my best for these people" mentality. Since our goal is to be strong men of character, this mentality simply will not do for us. By the way, the answer to the question "Why should I do my best for these people?" is and always will be, "Because my best is what I expect from myself." It's called work ethic, and it is about how you carry yourself in the workplace. You cannot control how other people act, but you can control how you respond to it. Also, don't forget that you are there to do a job, not to make friends.

One thing that helped me throughout my entire work history was that my expectations for myself have always exceeded those of any boss I have ever worked for, but not because I wanted to impress the boss. I always knew I expected more from myself than the boss ever could.

Along with the mind-set to always set your self-expectations high, you can never give thought to the idea of doing just enough to get by. *Life Lesson:* Doing just good enough is never good enough. Always strive for self-excellence. Always give your very best and then some. The last thing you want is to be known as the guy who just does enough to get by. Even worse than the just-enough guy is the lazy guy. These guys are just taking up oxygen and space. They also spend more energy trying to get out of work rather than just doing the job.

Since we are on the subject of expectations, I would recommend that whenever you start a new job or get a new boss, ask that person what his or her expectations of you are. Then you will know for sure what you need to do to exceed. It will show initiative on your part and open the door for further communication.

Speaking of communication, if your boss gives you direction to complete a task and you are unsure what you need to do, I strongly suggest that you ask for clarification before you do it wrong. However, if six months down the road you are still asking the same questions, the boss is going to think something is wrong with you.

"Whatever you do, do your work heartily, as for the Lord rather than for men."
—*Colossians 3:23*

Professionalism

Always, always, and another always conduct yourself in a professional manner while at work. I don't care if the boss is hardly ever around and everyone at work acts like a bunch of idiots, you still need to conduct yourself in a professional manner. It goes back to you expecting the best from yourself. I also don't care if you get so angry that smoke is coming out of your ears; control yourself and act professionally. Even if you get angry because of something someone else has done to you, you still need be professional. If you act unprofessionally, it may well be viewed differently. Fair or unfair, it will be seen as the actions of an "angry black man," and that's what will be remembered. Never forget that we are all accountable for our actions. Don't let the actions of others bring you down. You can never afford the comfort of not thinking before you act in life, and that includes work.

It is okay to enjoy your job and to have fun at work; just remember that is not the reason you are there. You are being paid to do a job, not to have fun. Learn accountability and fairness (or lack thereof) now. Just because Billy, your white coworker, gets away with something, it does not mean that you will too. Things may have changed somewhat since I first entered the workforce. However, I know one thing hasn't changed, and that is that men of color can't be just as good as our white counterparts; we have to be better. No, it's not fair, but it is a reality, so conduct yourself accordingly. Again, always assume you are being watched. That doesn't mean that people are looking for you to mess up, as it can also mean that you are being watched in terms of your job performance and potential for advancement. Either way, always conduct yourself as though you are being watched because you are.

It is always best to keep your personal life and work life separate. With that said, here is some food for thought regarding dating people at work. Let's say you start dating a woman you met on the job, and everything is super cool for a couple of months. Then for some reason, things go bad, and I mean really bad. Now you have to go to work with this woman who hates the very sight of you. To top it off, all your personal and intimate business is all over the workplace. God help you if you start seeing another woman at work. Now you have double trouble. Also, since you work at the same place, she could claim that you are sexually harassing her, and it would be your word against hers. Word to the wise: keep work and your personal life separate.

Being professional includes showing up to work on time; just to be safe, make a habit of being early. It also includes being reliable, dependable, and trustworthy. Here is some more insider information for the workplace and life. If you make a habit of always doing the right thing, you will spend a lot less time looking over your shoulder because you won't have to worry about things popping up as you have nothing to hide. I'm not saying it will be easy, but it is a good mind-set to have. Last, even when you leave one job for another, do it in a professional manner. Never burn bridges because you never know when you may need to cross them again. Even when you quit a job because you were treated unfairly, give your managers proper notice. Don't cuss them out and tear stuff up on your way out. Nothing is worse than interviewing for a position you really want and finding that the first person you see on the other side of the table is the person you called everything but a child of God many years earlier.

Know the Rules

Get to know your job. Most of the time when you start a new job, the boss will hook you up with an experienced person to help you learn the ropes. Sometimes that person may have been around a while, but that does not mean he or she is the best person to be training others. He or she may be teaching you the easiest way and not necessarily the correct way of doing things. So always go in with your eyes wide open and your mouth closed, unless you have a question. Make sure you find out the policies and procedures for your job. Read them and know them for yourself, not just what somebody told you because that might not be accurate. I like to call this knowing the rules of the game. The better you know the rules and abide by them, the better chance you have of hanging around. Whenever you make up rules on your own, you increase your chances for failure.

Whenever I had a new assignment either as an employee or as an employer, I would always go in and watch to see what was really going on. I would ask a few questions, but mainly I just observed. You learn so much more when your mouth is closed and your eyes and ears are open. People's mouths can tell you anything, but their actions always speak loudest.

Here are a few other things that you may want to take along with you. Never forget that your job is what you do to pay the bills, but it does not define who you are. If you forget that and for whatever reason lose your job, you have not only lost your income but your self-identity as well. If you are a busboy or a janitor, that is only your job title. Your title has nothing to do with what type of man you are; that is defined by your character.

When I was still working in the prison and had just been promoted to lieutenant, I went to dinner with my friend and his wife. After dinner, my friend's wife asked me a question that totally caught me off guard, but it made me think. I have never forgotten the question and have used it the rest of my career to support my philosophy of never letting your job title define who you are. The question she asked me was, "Are you going to be a black lieutenant, or are you going to be a lieutenant who is black?" I still think that was an awesome question. After letting it sink in for a few seconds, I told her, "I am a black lieutenant because, first and foremost, I am a black man whose job title just happens to be lieutenant." Be who you are first. You make the titles; don't let the titles make you. When I was born, my mother named me Charles, and when I die, I will still be just Charles. Yes, I have had some cool titles along the way, but thoses titles are not what make me who I am.

I recently read a list of ten things that require absolutely zero talent in

127

the workplace. I didn't create this list, but it surely goes along with what we have been talking about in this chapter. Lock these away in your brain as they will definitely come in handy down the road.

1. Being on time
2. Work ethic
3. Effort
4. Body language
5. Energy
6. Attitude
7. Passion
8. Being teachable
9. Doing extra
10. Being prepared.

"In all labor there is profit, but mere talk leads only to poverty."
—*Proverbs 14:23*

Finances

I am far from being a financial expert but during my journey I had to find out some hard lessons regarding money, lessons that I wish someone would have told me about long ago. In this section, we are going to talk a little about the things I learned that I hope will help you. We are going to discuss general, foundational things, so no investing or building stock portfolios here.

Because I started working at an early age and we were poor, I knew the value of money. Money was hard to come by, so the last thing I wanted to do was waste it. When I was working at KFC, I think the minimum wage was not even three dollars an hour, but it was still big money to me and I earned it honestly. At the early age of fourteen, the important things to me were buying my own clothes and saving for a car, and I did both. I got to keep my clothes, but Mom snatched the car when I thought I was a little too grown.

Because I had real-world family responsibilities at age nineteen, my thoughts regarding finances totally changed. While I wholeheartedly valued my time in the navy, make no mistake about it, the service is not there to make you rich. So with a family of four depending on me, I had to quickly learn what budgeting was and how to make it work.

Budget

A budget is nothing more than a plan for properly managing the money you have coming in and going out. Say you only have one thousand dollars coming in per month. That means you need to write out your expenditures (money going out), which include your bills such as rent, electricity, water, car, insurance, food, gas, and so on. You don't have to be a mathematical genius to know that it does not take long for that one thousand dollars to go out much faster than it came in.

Budgeting takes discipline (another one of those character traits) to work. It is important that you commit early on to operate within your budget. When you operate outside of your budget, be prepared to have some added stress in your life. Budget discipline starts with actually taking the time to write out your expenditures to help you stay focused and on track. Here is a classic example of a bad budget: You just got paid and cashed your check, and now, as my mom used to say, "That money is burning a hole in your pocket." So the first thing you do is buy that pair of Jordans you have been drooling over all month. Then you buy a new stereo for your car since only the radio is working. Now you finally make it home, and you decide it's time to pay your bills. Of course, you don't have enough money because you had zero financial discipline.

In establishing a budget, it is important that you understand the big differences between wants and needs. You have to set your priorities and stick with it. Your needs are your priorities; they include things like a place to live, gas in your car so you can get to work, electricity so you can see, and of course food.

Wants are things that are nice to have but are not vital to survival. Setting priorities involves making sure your needs are taken care of before you even think about wants. To do this, I strongly suggest you incorporate the "pay before you play" method of budgeting. All that means is that before you spend anything from your check, make sure you pay your bills before you play. This method will help you maintain discipline and ensure that you don't blow your money on wants and not take care of your priorities (needs). I know this may sound extremely basic, but you would be surprised how many people my age have yet to grasp this concept. The earlier you understand this, the better off you will be in the long run. You can incorporate it into your responsible character.

Setting budgetary priorities is not fun, which is why you are going to have to learn how to deny yourself the things you want so you can get the things you need. Remember, discipline takes practice, and it needs to be nurtured. This type of self-discipline training will also reflect itself in other parts of your life as well. Once you know you can deny yourself in financial matters, you will feel confident that you can do the same in other areas of your life, such as saying no to yourself when faced with doing things you know you shouldn't do. There is a saying that goes, "A fool and his money are soon parted." Don't be foolish in the handling of your finances.

Credit

Credit is something I had no clue about when I started out, and I had to learn some tough lessons. In the previous section (budgeting), I mentioned that operating outside your budget is when you get yourself in trouble. Misuse of credit is a primary path to getting yourself outside your budget.

Before we get too deep into this, let's start off by saying that, whenever possible it is always better to pay cash for things rather than using credit to attain them. I was going to put that last part all in capital letters, but I didn't want you to feel like I was yelling at you. I cannot stress this fact enough: credit gives you a false sense of having extra money. This false sense results from having a credit card in your pocket that is not maxed out, and you tend to think you have extra cash in your pocket. That simply is not the truth. The people who have your money in their pocket are the credit card companies. Take, for example, the businesses that give you a loan until you get paid. They will gladly loan you money, but please know that you are going to pay it back *plus interest*. Once you get on that merry-go-round, it is incredibly hard to get off of it.

Always try to pay cash for something whenever possible. It will really test your discipline, goal setting, and planning. For example, you know that sometime soon you are going to need new tires for your car. Your goal is to pay cash for the tires because you now know you always pay more when you buy things on credit. So your goal is set, which for the record is a need. Now you plan by finding out how much the tires will cost so you know exactly how much to save to purchase them. On a related side note, when you get the tires, stay disciplined and focused—only get the tires. The tires are a need, but the new shiny wheels the shop is offering you on credit are not.

Another negative with credit is that your financial sins in your youth can come back and bite you in the butt down the road. The credit card companies don't tell you that since it is their job to get as much money out of you as possible. The credit card companies are a lot like a Las Vegas slot machine. They both give you a little money on the front end, but the ultimate goal is to get all of it back plus extra on the back end.

Credit card companies really don't care about you being young and financially immature. They may still give you one, two, or three cards. Then you will have that false sense of security of having extra money in your pocket. Before you know it, all of the cards are maxed out, and of course you can't pay it back because you are operating way outside your budget.

A credit history report is a tracking instrument that is used to keep track of your bill pay history. Your level or grade of credit is called a credit score, and it determines what level of trustworthiness other creditors will determine you have. Even if you don't have a credit card but have been negligent in paying certain bills, like those for electricity and other utilities, that can also show up on your credit report. This may mean absolutely nothing to you right now, but trust me—it will get your full attention later as you advance into the real world.

Those credit cards that you didn't pay when you were eighteen years old are going to seriously haunt you later in your early twenties and beyond. Here are a few examples of how poor credit can haunt you. Let's say your car is on its last leg, and you need another one. You go to the new car dealer, and the salespeople are all smiles and overly friendly until they run your credit report, which reveals all of your unpaid credit cards and late payments for numerous other bills. You are almost laughed off the new car lot because your credit report indicates that you are an extreme credit risk. Next, you strut on over to the used car lot, and the same thing happens all over again. There are a few used car lots that specialize in extreme risks like you, but they're going to charge you beyond-crazy interest rates (more on this in a bit). Also, your monthly car note is going to be ridiculously high. Bad credit will even haunt you when you try to rent an apartment and be a nightmare when you get ready to purchase a home, and it can also haunt you on certain jobs. Some employers will run your credit history to get a feel for your character. They figure that if you aren't responsible enough to handle your finances, how can you be a responsible employee?

Something as small as a late or nonpayment can have much greater consequences (there's that word again) later down the road. Take heed, young men, and know that the best way to avoid a credit crisis is to plan in advance. You not only need a plan, but you must also put the plan into action to avoid getting into a negative situation in the first place. Knowing means nothing if you don't act on what you know. That's how applied knowledge becomes power—knowing then doing.

Personally, I learned about credit the hard way—not necessarily because I had bad credit but because I simply didn't have any credit history. When I started my young family, I didn't have any credit at all. I tried to establish credit by applying for credit cards, but I got shot down every time. That is when I learned that it takes credit to get credit. I know it doesn't make sense, but it is a reality.

My first experience with credit was a prepaid credit card. That meant my credit limit was based on the amount of money I put on the card. If I didn't have any money to put on the card, it was useless. I used that to get my foot into the credit world. My next form of credit was a vacuum cleaner. It was a very good vacuum, but that was not the only reason I bought it. I did need a vacuum but not for the price the thing cost me back then. I bought it because the store was willing to sell me something on credit, and I was trying to establish my credit.

I know I told you to purchase as much as you can with cash, but remember that I am sharing the lessons I learned. I also understand that there will be times when you just won't have cash readily available and will need to establish credit. I am primarily talking about big-ticket items like vehicles and someday a home.

Later, when I had a good job and a decent credit history, I again applied for and received a regular credit card. I remember feeling pretty proud of myself and thinking I was finally on my way to financial respectability. However, in my ignorance, I didn't know a thing about the interest rates of a credit card. I must have thought that I would just pay back what I charged to the card. I never thought of interest rates. I found out the hard way that all credit cards are not created equal. I simply had no clue.

I went with the first company that was willing to issue me a card. The first real card I had had an interest rate close to 25 percent, meaning that not only was I paying back whatever I used the card for but an additional 25 percent on the remaining balance. Being Mr. Responsible, I always made sure I paid my bill promptly, but it never really seemed like my bill was going down. That's because I was only paying the minimum payment, which, in turn, helped keep the balance high, and that kept the interest charges high. That was a hard lesson to learn.

Be very careful with how you utilize credit. Know that credit cards can be a very enticing trap, so proceed with much caution. Be very aware of interest rates on anything you buy. There is a huge difference in paying 5 percent interest and paying 25 percent. Pay more than the minimum payments on credit cards because all it does is keep the credit card companies rich on those inflated balances. Know that with a credit card in hand, you will have much more temptation on purchasing wants and not taking care of needs. Don't forget that bad credit history will come back to haunt you as you mature and start making better financial decisions. Be of responsible character and very mindful of your finances.

Here are a few closing comments regarding finances. First, just know that Uncle Sam (the US Government) does not play when it comes to paying your taxes. If you owe taxes, pay them and do so quickly because Uncle Sam can and will take your future earnings. If the Internal Revenue Service is coming after you, they can fine you, put a freeze on your assets, and in extreme cases send you to prison. As I got older and wiser in the CDC, I made sure to adjust my tax withholding to have the maximum taken out from the start. I would much rather they owe me than I owe them.

Second, I know this is hard to do when sometimes you may just be making it from paycheck to paycheck, but when things stabilize a bit, try to get in the habit of saving a certain amount of your check. One way of doing that is that, when you get a raise, you can either put all or half of the amount of the raise into savings. The reasoning behind that is since you were already accustomed to making a certain amount, the raise is extra, so put it away before you get used to the new amount.

Last, earlier I used an example of how to make a budget work. I used the income amount of a thousand dollars per month. That example was based on just you taking care of yourself. So think how much harder that becomes when you have to take care of a wife or girlfriend and kids with the same amount of money. Add child support to the mix of money coming out of your pocket if you have children from a previous relationship. Then again, you won't have to worry about child support coming out your pocket because it will get taken out of your check before you even see it. Now that's some serious food for thought. I want you to think about that before getting married or getting you're a girl pregnant. Young men, think, plan, and act accordingly.

"He who tills his land will have plenty of bread, but he who pursues worthless things lacks sense."
—Proverbs 12:11

CHAPTER 8

LEADERSHIP

In this chapter, we are going to talk about a few aspects of leadership and what it means to lead. What do you think of when you hear the word *leader*? Most think of someone being in charge of large groups of people. You might think of the president of the United States or a chairman of a large company. You may think of those in charge of military forces like a general in the army or an admiral in the navy. Perhaps some of you think of sports team coaches when you think about leaders. Any and all of those are correct. However, there are so many more types of leaders that you see every day that may not be high profile but are every bit as important.

Leadership has to do with people. I strongly believe that the best leaders are the people who truly care about the people they lead. I don't mean that they vaguely care but that they have whole-hearted compassion for those of whom they are in charge and lead. True leaders are more concerned about the well-being of those in their care than they are for themselves.

Those who claim to be leaders tend to get themselves in trouble when they put their personal desires ahead of those they lead. When this happens, they either forgot or never knew that a true leader is first and foremost there to serve the needs of the people. When leaders fail to understand that the needs of those they lead and serve are greater than their individual needs, their focus, mission, and purpose can become lost. Their focus becomes how something can best serve their own needs. A quote by Dr. Cornell West best describes what I am talking about: "You can't lead the people if you don't love the people. You can't save the people if you don't serve the people."

To be an effective leader, it is important you care for and serve those you lead. If this is your focus, it will help you stay on track and not get stuck on yourself. I believe this is a major problem that plagues our nation today. We have so-called leaders who are more concerned about their own agendas, power, fame, or financial gain than about truly looking out for the people. As a nation, we need more leaders and fewer politicians. We need leaders who not only do things right but do the right thing.

Remember earlier when I told you that life is much more than all about you? It's a concept I believe has not been fully embraced by those in charge of leading our country. These people are more concerned about doing whatever it takes to attain certain political positions than meeting the needs of the people. We will forever be adrift as long as our leaders don't commit to doing the right thing.

Leadership is defined as "the position or function of a leader, a person who guides or directs a group." At a local level, the leaders in your community are your teachers, parents, guardians, pastors, coaches, and so on.

There are leaders and followers in every social group. If you are a part of any sports group, formal or informal, I am sure you know the individuals the group will look to for direction. The same is true for your group of friends or associates. That person may even be you. Hopefully, by the time we get to the end of this chapter, you will be able to identify some qualities and characteristics of an effective leader.

The truth of the matter is that not everyone is cut out to be a leader, nor is everyone comfortable in that role. Problems arise not because you are a follower but when you follow blindly. I define a blind follower as one who simply goes along without question or opposition just to get along with a particular group. Blind followers will go along even when they know they are being led in the wrong direction because they believe it is easier to go along than it is to ask questions or just say no. Not everyone can be the leader, but you do get to choose whom you follow. An example of this would be when you are hanging out with your friends and the leader decides everyone is going to do something you know will get you into big trouble. However, instead of speaking up, you simply go along with the plan. That's being a blind follower who has chosen to go along to get along.

I have been a leader and I have been one who follows as well, but I have never been a blind follower. Regardless of who the leader may be, he has at one time or another been a follower. As a follower, I have learned many great things that I have adopted as I have evolved and found my own leadership style. I have learned to observe leaders for their effective traits and characteristics. However, while making these observations, I have also learned what traits were least effective and would not work for me. (They didn't really work for them either.)

Regarding observations, when you are looking at the leadership traits of others, it is important to know that just because a particular style worked for someone else, it doesn't mean it will work for you. To be an effective leader, you need to be genuine in the leading of others. Nothing is worse than leaders trying to be someone or something they are not. If you find yourself in the role of leader, find and cultivate your own leadership style. Be real; your style needs to reflect your personality. If you are a warm, outgoing, and cheery kind of person, don't adopt the style of a straight-to-the-point, hard-butt, no-BS type of leader. Those who follow you will see right through the image you are trying to portray.

It is important that you know that just because you are in the role of a leader does not mean you will not make mistakes. You *will* make mistakes, and because you are the leader, everyone will notice them. Don't try to hide them; own them and learn the lesson they teach. Leaders are human, and humans make mistakes. When you try to act perfect, people will be hesitant to follow you completely because they will not see you as a real person. As a leader, some of my most valuable lessons have come from making mistakes. I am a person who hates to make mistakes, but I am a realist and know that I am far from perfect. When I make a mistake, I own it and vow to learn from it in hopes of never repeating it.

I have said this before, but it is worth repeating: A mistake does not have to be yours for you to learn from it. If you see or hear about someone else making a mistake, learn from it. Don't think you are smarter than the person who made the mistake. So what happened to him can't possibly happen to you, right? Plenty of people are locked up in prison who had that same mentality.

> *"Those who have insight will shine brightly like the brightness of the expanse of heaven, and those who lead the many to righteousness, like the stars forever and ever."*
> —*Daniel 12:3*

Things to Look for in a Good Leader

There are numerous character traits that go into the making of a good leader. We won't talk about them all, but we will discuss a few that I believe should be at or near the top of the list. Seek these traits out should you find yourself in a leadership role, or look for them in those you follow.

To be an effective leader, a person must have integrity. We talked about this much earlier when we discussed character traits. The best leaders are those with strong moral and ethical principles. Being a leader who consistently does the right thing is a breath of fresh air to those being led.

This next leadership trait goes hand in hand with having integrity, and that is the willingness and ability to lead by example. By now, you are well aware that I am big on letting your actions speak for you. How can you be an effective leader in battle if you tell your soldiers to be brave, but your actions show signs of cowardice? How can you be an effective political leader when you talk about how much integrity you have, but your actions clearly show you can be bought for a price? How can you be a church leader when you preach on Christ-like qualities, but your actions are visibly contrary to the words you speak? These are just a few examples. If you are going to lead others, then demonstrate the behavior you want those who follow you to copy. True leadership is a huge responsibility and should not be taken lightly. If you want to lead or follow the best leaders, ensure that their actions match their words and that their actions support the example they set.

We have already talked about this next trait in this chapter, but I felt the need to include it in this list. To be an effective leader, you must truly care about those whom you lead. How can you be a good leader if your mind-set is, "What's best for me?" Your own agenda clearly outweighs the needs of those you lead.

To be an effective leader, a person needs to possess a determined and positive attitude. No one wants to follow a person whose life outlook is nothing but doom and gloom. Life is filled with plenty of dark moments. We need our leaders to inspire us with positivity. Even when things are at their worst, point to the positive and remind the people that things can and will get better.

Confidence is a must-have trait for an effective leader to possess. I am talking about real confidence, not the fake made-up macho stuff. I'm talking about a type of belief in oneself that others can sense when you enter a room. And it's not only a belief in yourself but also in the people you serve—not cockiness or arrogance. Arrogance is self-serving because arrogant people want life to be all about them. A sign of a humble leader is that when things are going well, he will praise others, not himself. Arrogant leaders will stand on the mountain and say, "Hey, everyone, look at me and see how great and amazing I am." No one wants to follow the arrogant leader. Nor do they want to follow a person who lacks confidence, wavers in their actions, and is indecisive. If you want people to believe in you, you must first believe in yourself.

A true leader stands up for or defends those unable to defend themselves. It is a quality to be fostered by a positive-minded leader who truly understands that it is his job and responsibility to look out for the well-being others. Remember when I mentioned that your talents, gifts, and abilities are not for you alone but for you to share with others? Do not ever get so big-headed that you think you are all that and that those who decide to follow you should be honored to have you as their great and awesome leader. Like I said before, life is about so much more than just you. If you have a gift of leadership, use that gift for the service of others, not simply so others can serve you.

If you see people being taken advantage of because they may not be strong or able to speak up for themselves, then stand up for them. Speak for those who have no voice. Don't do it because it shines a light on your own perceived greatness but because it is the right thing to do. Selfish-minded leaders will utilize their leadership gift for personal gain. Because of their self-serving mentality, they will bully and oppress those they should be representing.

An effective leader will need courage to stand alone if need be for the sake of doing the right thing. True leadership is not all about being in the spotlight and taking full credit for the hard work of others. It is easy to take the credit when everything is going smoothly and fine. Real leaders will find out who they truly are when they are in the face of adversity, when everybody appears to be against them. When this happens, stand fast and do the right thing even when it is tempting to take the easy way out.

This type of stand will take real courage, the type of courage that requires doing the right thing in the face of adversity. I'm talking about courage, not stubbornness just for the sake of having to be right. Yes, there is a huge difference. Courage is what it takes to stand up for others. Like arrogance, stubbornness is self-serving and does not serve the people.

It will also take courage to accept a difficult challenge instead of taking the easy road. As a leader, will your decisions benefit those you lead, or will they only benefit you? Which road would you choose? That is a trick question. Of course, as an effective leader who cares, you would make the right choices because it is in the best interest of the people you lead.

It also takes courage to make difficult and unpopular decisions. Know this—as a leader you are never going to please everyone. However, if you are a man of integrity and character, you will strive to make sound well-thought-out decisions that are for the collective good of those you lead. The role of a leader can and will get very lonely at times. These times will require courage, conviction, and focus on doing the right thing for those you lead even if they don't know it at the time. You will often have the input of others in making the difficult, unpopular decisions, which is a good thing, but at the end of the day it is ultimately your responsibility.

It will also take courage to fight the fear of failure. As a leader, you will need to be decisive. You will need to make tough decisions. No one likes to fail at anything, and that includes leaders when it comes to making tough decisions. As a leader, it is easy to put unrealistic expectations on yourself. Remember that just because you are a leader, it does not mean you are no longer human and that you will no longer make mistakes. It simply means you are a person who is responsible for the well-being of others.

You cannot let the fear of making a bad decision freeze you from actually making a decision. Gather as much information as you can. Look at it from every possible angle, seek input from those you trust (being a leader does not mean you know everything), and make the call. The reality is that in life you are not going to get it right every time. When you make a bad call, learn from the mistake and move on.

Successful leaders are not people who have never failed. They are the people who had the courage to get up and keep fighting. Successful leaders just don't know how to quit. The fear of failure is far more damaging than failure itself. If you let it, the fear of failure will make you indecisive and unable to act in the time of need. It will also make you choose the easy road instead of the right one. Like I said, there are many more attributes that make up an effective leader. These are the ones I looked for in those I followed and expected from myself as a leader.

> *"Do nothing from selfishness or empty conceit, but with humility of mind regard one another as more important than yourselves. Do not merely look out for your own personal interests, but also for the interest of others."*
> *—Philippians 2:3–4*

Positive and Negative Leaders

It is important to know that not all leaders are of the positive type. Just as we are all born with different talents, gifts, and abilities, it is up to us to choose what we do with them. That is why it is vital to choose wisely whom you follow. Not all leaders have your best interest in mind. I am a firm believer that some people are indeed natural-born leaders. However, I also believe that people can learn to lead. Just because a person is born with the ability to lead, it does not mean they will choose to use their gifts for the betterment of others. The negative type will use their gifts to manipulate others for their own selfish agendas. Positive and negative leaders are all around us on a daily basis, but it is up to us to recognize them and decide whether to follow them.

My favorite leader in history is Jesus because He loved those whom He led and served, even to the point of dying for them. There's no greater love than that. I also love that He not only told the people how they should act, but He demonstrated the ultimate standard of leading by example.

Jesus' actions supported His words, but the Son of God may be a tough example to follow. Another example of an exemplary leader was Dr. Martin Luther King. What impresses me about Dr. King is that he spoke for those with no voice. He stood for righteousness, he loved the people, and he set the example for how to carry ourselves in the face of extreme adversity. He didn't need to say, "Hey, I'm the leader of my people." It was obvious to those who followed him and to those who hated and eventually killed him for the cause he led.

An example of an extreme yet effective negative leader was Adolf Hitler. This man took the gifts, talents, and abilities that he was born with and used them to convince an entire nation to support his hateful agenda—an agenda that led to the deaths of millions.

Whether or not you agree with the leadership of Jesus, Dr. King, or Hitler, the fact is that they were powerful, history-making, life-changing leaders. There are many others, but I think you get the point. It is up to you to recognize both the positive and negative leaders. Choose very carefully whom you will follow. In some cases, it can mean the difference between life and death. Again, do not follow anyone or anything blindly. Be wise and take the time to make the right decision because you will have to live with the consequences of your choice.

Before we move on, I need to provide you with another example of a negative leader. While working inside CDC's prisons, I was witness to some pretty dynamic leaders who happened to be inmates. These men living with the consequences of their decisions chose to use their natural-born leadership skills for their own selfish ambitions and agendas. Their agendas usually revolved around power and financial gain. However, their agendas were usually disguised as something noble, like the betterment of a particular group, such as those focused on gang affiliation or racial pride. However, in the end, it always came down to power and money. You see, these negative leaders cared for those they led but only as long as they served a purpose to them. These leaders rarely served the needs of others. People only existed to serve their needs.

Manipulation of the followers was accomplished by many methods, to include fear, intimidation, and intellectual influence. These negative leaders were able to get hundreds and even thousands of inmates, most of whom they had never met, to carry out severe criminal acts, even murder, in the name of a cause determined by the negative leader.

For example, a powerful leader who is doing life without the possibility of parole is locked up in the segregated housing unit (maximum lock-up) in Pelican Bay State Prison near the California-Oregon border. This leader decides an inmate within the group (gang) needs to be murdered for whatever reason, so he sends the word out to have the murder committed as part of his own power-driven agenda.

The person who is chosen to carry out the murder is near the end of his sentence and will be getting out of prison soon, but he commits the murder as ordered. He gets caught and convicted, and he is given a new sentence of twenty-five years to life. So now this young man who went to prison with a sentence of two years for stealing a car is most likely never getting out of prison because he chose to follow and let another person dictate his actions. You tell me—does the powerful leader at Pelican Bay care about the person he ordered to commit the homicide? Of course not, because it does not affect him at all, even if authorities find out that the leader was the one who gave the order for the murder. What can you do to a person who is never getting out of prison anyway? The person who carried out the murder was nothing more than a mere puppet for the leader, furthering his agenda of maintaining power and controlling others with fear and intimidation.

Granted, these are some pretty serious examples of positive and negative leadership, but they are intended to show you the importance of recognizing the types of leaders you desire to be or follow. Young men, it still comes down to your being critical thinkers instead of just following blindly. Always ask yourself, *Does this person have my best interests in mind?* If the answer is no, then obviously you are following the wrong person.

I now believe that I was born with strong leadership qualities. Most of my life, I found myself thrust into leadership positions, from being the oldest child to my KFC, navy, and CDC days. It seemed I was often in charge of something or someone. A coworker and friend of mine came up a phrase that I think applies to me: "a reluctant leader." To me, the phrase fits me perfectly because I didn't really seek out leadership, but if I was put in that position, you could be sure I was going to carry out the task to the best of my ability.

That reminds me of another point I mentioned earlier about not letting titles define who you are. I am not impressed by titles; however, I am impressed by true character. In my career, I have encountered many people of poor character with high-ranking, impressive-sounding titles. Impressive titles don't make impressive people. Some of the best natural-born leaders whom I have known were not high-ranking; they were first-line staff. These people didn't have to order their staff around because of their titles. These leaders led others by their actions and character. Their actions, not their words, spoke volumes about who they were. Something about them just made me want to listen to what they had to say. These are the people I watched and emulated. The one thing they all had in common was that they truly cared about people.

Just because people have impressive titles does not mean they are leaders. It can simply mean they got jobs that gave them the titles. They may even be in charge, but true leaders will never have to tell you, "I'm the leader." If you pay attention, you will see and know who the real leaders are.

> *"For You are my rock and my fortress; For Your name's sake You will lead me and guide me."*
> —*Psalm 31:3*

Responsibility of Leadership

Leaders will accept responsibility for unfavorable outcomes and will share praise for the favorable ones. True leaders will always seek opportunities to put the spotlight on those they serve rather than themselves. It may sound easy, but it is contrary to human behavior. The norm is that when things go bad, most people are quick to point fingers at others. However, as a leader, you are not only responsible for what you do but also for the actions of those you lead. That may not sound fair, but that is what sets apart the person who just wants the title of boss and a true leader. Pay attention to the news and watch for those leaders who accept responsibility for their actions and those who are quick to point fingers at someone else.

The responsibility of leadership can at times be a heavy burden, which is why it is not for everyone. Leadership is much more than desiring to be the boss. It is a responsibility that shouldn't be taken lightly because it affects the lives of others.

As a leader, it is also your responsibility to inspire and build others up, not to tear them down because you are in the position to do so. To build others up, you must care. That is the major difference between a positive and a negative leader. Since a positive leader cares about those whom they lead, he will be more apt to build others up. Negative leaders will tend to tear people down because of their need to feel powerful. Positive leaders understand the importance of building others up and will always look for ways to do so. If the leader truly cares about people, then inspiring others will come naturally. To the contrary, negative leaders who have an "it's all about me" mentality will have a difficult time inspiring others because they feel it will take the spotlight off of themselves.

Everyday Leaders

The purpose of this chapter was to help you understand a few finer points of leadership, as well as to ensure that you can recognize the positive and negative qualities of those who lead so you can copy those of a positive leader and avoid those of a negative nature.

While some of the concepts I discussed may appear grand and high level, they are important and applicable to you. One day you may be responsible for large-scale leadership. Never sell yourself short. You never know what is in store for you, so continue to strive to evolve and grow. Second, the concepts and traits I have discussed are the same regardless of the level of leadership you find yourself.

The most important thing I want you to take away from this chapter is that not only high-profile people are important leaders. It's the people right alongside you to whom you can reach out who are the most important leaders. These are people like our teachers, coaches, religious leaders, friends, and of course family. The list goes on. You see, it doesn't make a difference if you lead one, ten, hundreds, or thousands of people, the traits outlined in this chapter still apply. The only thing that changes is the number of those you lead.

Everyone is a leader in his or her own way. Our communities need you, either now or in the future, to step up and lead our children, not just make them and leave them to raise themselves. You may think of the president of the United States when I say *leader*, but the most important leader in the life of a child should be the father. Our communities are hurting for many reasons, but a main reason is that our fathers are missing in action.

We need our men to teach, guide, love, and lead our children in the way they should go. Men of color need to step up and lead our women as well. The black woman is the strongest female on this planet, not by choice but out of necessity. A black woman will do what she has to in order to take care of her children. Too often in our communities, they have led the way because our men are not accepting and embracing their roles as protectors and leaders of our women and children.

To be a black male in America is not easy, by any means. However, just because it's been hard for us as a people does not take away the responsibility of our men leading our families. In case you haven't noticed, it is terribly hard for black women as well. However, they find a way to adapt and overcome, and they have been doing so for hundreds of years in this country. They don't do it to minimize our role as fathers, husbands, and men but because they couldn't always depend on us in general.

We men of today and you young men of tomorrow must do a better job of being leaders of our communities, our homes, and ourselves. To lead others, you must first be able to lead yourself. Leading yourself means making good, well-thought-out choices and decisions. Fathers, lead your children by first setting the example. Stop being a blind follower who goes along with the crowd. Stand up for what's right even if you have to do it alone and say no to the crowd. We are all leaders in one way or another, even if you're simply leading yourself. Stand up and be your own man. Don't lead others astray, and don't let others lead you off course.

"Lead me in Your truth and teach me, For You are the God of my salvation, For You, I wait all the day."
—*Psalm 25:5*

CHAPTER 9

SOCIAL ISSUES

Young men there are several more real-life subjects we still need to discuss. As with everything else we have been discussing, the following subjects are things you need to consider seriously. I will not tell you what to do since we all have to make our own choices and decisions. However, I strongly suggest that you never forget the PC+BD=NC equation and that you are the one who has to live with the consequences of your decisions and actions. There is much to discuss, so let's get started.

Courtesy, Common Respect, and Good Manners

I'm going to start this one off with a couple of quick personal experiences to get my point across. The first one happened to me many years ago. I was driving home after work at the prison, eager to get out of my uniform. I was about three miles from home when I stopped at a red light. There was a young girl, who just happened to be white, in the car directly in front of me.

The light changed, but the girl was not paying attention. I waited for about three seconds, and then I honked my horn to get her attention. I saw her snap her head up as if startled. She then looked at me in her rearview mirror, flipped me off, and then proceeded through the light. I admit that her blatant show of disrespect surprised and angered me. Unfortunately for this young girl, I just happened to be heading in the same direction as her. I could see she was getting very nervous because this angry-looking black man appeared to be following her. She finally turned off the street we had been traveling, and I just looked at her as I drove past. Maybe the look wasn't exactly warm and fuzzy, but it was just a look. I didn't even return the single-finger salute she had given me at the light.

I couldn't help but think that this girl had no clue as to how lucky she was. I know a lot of people who would have gone off on her. She was lucky that it was me she had flipped off and not some of my folks from the other side of town. Due to my occupation and the color of my skin, I was the one who had to keep my composure. Otherwise, more than likely, I would have been the one in trouble. There's nothing fair about it, but it's reality all the same.

It still bothered me that this girl had the nerve to respond in such a disrespectful manner. Was it because she was a young white girl and I was black? Was it because she was young and ignorant and had not been taught to show respect to her elders? I am sure it was probably a combination of both.

The second event took place many years later while I was living and working in the Bay Area. One night, my wife and I went to a local movie theater to check out the latest Denzel Washington film. I admit I was not in the best of moods that evening, and I probably should have kept my butt at home. About a minute after sitting down, I felt the person behind me forcefully kicking the back of my seat. I let it go for a bit just to make sure it wasn't an accident, but the person continued doing it. I finally realized it wasn't going to stop, so I turned around and saw a young man who appeared to be Hispanic and around seventeen years old. I calmly asked him, "Could you please stop kicking my seat?" I gave him the benefit of the doubt; perhaps he didn't realize he was kicking the seat.

His response totally caught me off guard. This dude told me as if it was a matter of common fact, "I was sitting here first." He said it as if that gave him to the right to act stupid and disrespectful. Things went downhill from there as I told him what I was about to do to him. It didn't get physical, but it was certainly heading in that direction. I think the young man realized he might have bitten off more than he could chew. Thank God for my wife, who got my attention and got me to take the high road and change seats.

I learned many things from these two situations. The main thing is the importance of thinking at all times, even more so when I am angry. In both cases, while I wasn't the one who started the trouble, had I acted without thought, it would have been me going to jail. It simply wasn't worth it.

While my anger was warranted in both situations, I would have still been held accountable for my actions. I had to remind myself of the consequences. No matter how I looked at it, I would have been the loser. Of course, I could have said, "There is no way I'm going to let them disrespect me," but in the end, would it really have been worth it? Again, this emphasizes the importance of thinking before acting.

Both stories do indeed reiterate the importance of thinking before you act, which is a bonus. But the reason I share these stories is to highlight youth's blatant acts of disrespect toward an elder. I grew up in a time when such acts of disrespect toward elders were nearly unheard of. In my day, the white girl would have gotten her butt whipped by her parents or the parents would have been cussed out for raising such a disrespectful child. The youngster in the theater would have simply gotten his butt beat right then and there, and no one would have said anything because he had it coming.

Some of you youngsters are saying, "Well, that was back in the day, old man." That may be true, but some things should be timeless, like common courtesy, respect, and the use of good manners. Do you really need to be taught how to treat people correctly?

For the most part, I do believe people need to be taught common courtesy, respect, and manners. At the very least, it needs to be witnessed, even from a distance, like on television. My mother taught me early on that lack of courtesy, disrespect of my elders, and the failure to use good manners would not be tolerated. Some of the things I'm talking about may appear old-fashioned, but please take them seriously and be a positive example to others.

Growing up, had I addressed an adult by his or her first name in the presence of my mother, I would have gotten a stinging backhand to the lips, just hard enough to remind me to show respect and address my elders as "Mr." or "Mrs." followed by their first or last name, depending on how close they were to the family. Of course, the use of *sir* or *ma'am* was always acceptable. When asked a question, I was expected to look the person in the eye and respond, "Yes, sir" or "Yes, ma'am." *Yeah, yep,* and *what* were not allowed.

If you didn't understand a question, you never said, "What?" The proper response was "Excuse me?" The question would be re-asked or rephrased if need be. When asking for something, you always included the word *please*, such as "Could I please have …?" Or if someone asked if you wanted something, the appropriate response was "Yes, please," immediately followed by "Thank you." A thank you shows respect and appreciation to the giver. Another big mistake was interrupting adults while they were speaking. If you needed to say something important, you would say, "Excuse me" and await permission to speak.

I know some of this stuff sounds basic to some of you, but I can't take it for granted that everyone knows. For those of you who already know, please let this serve as a reminder to not only know but use these courtesies. If they are new to you, no problem—just start putting them into practice.

I think part of the problem is that some young men today think that courtesies such as showing respect and using manners are a sign of weakness. Some may even think it means they are trying to act white. Both mentalities are quite untrue. In fact, it takes confidence to carry yourself in the right manner despite what others may think. I was taught these things early in life, and they have stayed with me to this day. It is my responsibility to pass them on to my children and grandchildren, and now I am sharing them with you.

Young men, the amount of money that you have or don't have has nothing to do with the use of good manners. When I was growing up, we didn't have a matching fork, spoon, or plate. However, Mom always made sure we knew and utilized good manners at whatever served as the dining room table (sometimes it was just a coffee table). We knew that we shouldn't eat with our elbows on the table, nor did we eat with our mouths open.

I remember times when Mom had saved enough money to expose us to eating in a restaurant. People would always compliment her on how well behaved her children were. She told us that we needed to know how to conduct ourselves in public so that we would never feel like there was somewhere we couldn't go. I never realized the significance of those compliments until I would get them with my own kids and now with my grandkids. The truth is that when I was a kid, we were afraid to act out in public. Mom had a rule that if we acted a fool in public, she would do the same and "handle the problem" right then and there. A well-mannered child is not only a reflection of the caregiver but is also a gift to society.

There is much more we could talk about in this area, but we have a lot of other things we need to discuss. Let me take a few minutes to talk about a few complaints I have on things that really bother me. Again, back in my day just like it is today, teenage boys used foul language when they were trying to act and talk tough. However, they only did that when they were among their buddies and very rarely around their elders. Talking like that around adults simply wasn't done since it was offensive not only to parents but to the entire neighborhood. If it did happen, the adult would tell your parents, and in some situations they had unspoken permission to smack you across the mouth. There's nothing like stinging lips for ten minutes to remind you to watch what you say and around whom you say it.

It's not that way today. I see and hear young men saying whatever pops into their heads, with absolutely no thought or concern for who is around them. If this is you and your buddies, please stop and show those around you some respect. Also, respect yourself and be considerate of others. How you carry yourself and act reflects your character.

Since we are talking about watching what you say, let's add one more thing. Young men, please stop addressing each other and others as "nigga." There is absolutely nothing positive about that term. The word "nigger" or "nigga" is deeply rooted to a time that we as a people are trying to move away from, not maintain. What is ironic is that we will want to do serious physical damage to a white person who uses the term, but we probably hold the most guilt for not allowing this word to die. If we want respect, then let's show some to ourselves by not demeaning ourselves.

Regardless of how much your clothes cost, ensure that they are neat and clean and that you are presentable to the world. Your appearance speaks for you way before you open your mouth. If you want to be respected, then respect yourself by caring about how you look in public. While you may not have two dollars in your pocket, that is no reason not to carry yourself like the king you were meant to be.

Young men, for the love of God, please buy and use a belt; stop this silly sagging stuff. There is a reason boxers and briefs are called *under*wear— it's because they are meant to be worn *under* your pants, not as an outer garment. Your underwear are not meant to be seen. The public doesn't want to see your drawers; that's a private matter, plus it looks real tacky. Enough said.

Another issue I have is when you get to a door ahead of a female, or anyone for that matter, the courteous thing to do is hold the door open for others before you enter. Do not just walk in and let the door close on the little old lady following you. Also, if someone holds a door for you, please be courteous and say thank you.

Last, be a gentleman. Learn to open and hold doors for your lady. Open and close the car door for her. Once you get to where you are going, get out and open her door to let her out of the car. Another point along the same line is when you go to a restaurant, pull out the chair for her to be seated. If your food comes first, do not start eating until she gets her food. You will find that courtesy, respect, and good manners will take you far and help you to stand out as a man of character.

> *"Listen to counsel and accept discipline, that you may be wise the rest of your days."*
>
> —*Proverbs 19:20*

Tolerance (Understanding Differences)

Lately, the term *tolerance* has been tossed around a lot, but what does it really mean? One source defines it as "a fair, objective, and permissive attitude toward those whose opinions, beliefs, practices, racial, or ethnic origins, etc., differ from one's own." Another definition of tolerance is "the ability to accept ideas, behaviors, and feelings that are different than those of the individual."

Somewhere along the line in today's society, if a person's point of view is not deemed socially correct by one group, he is considered intolerant or negative. One of the primary themes in this book is that life is about you making your own choices. That includes the choice to think for yourself and hopefully make good decisions. By now I hope you understand that although you made a choice, it does not mean you are exempt from the consequences of that choice or decision. That is why I stress the importance of being real thinkers, not just doers and blind followers.

Ultimately, it is you who decides how you think and act. We are all different; no two people think exactly alike, and there is nothing wrong with that. We need to understand that just because someone does not agree with us on a particular subject does not mean that person is wrong.

It simply means they have a contrary point of view and their thoughts are different than ours. Having a different point of view by itself does not necessarily make anyone a bad person.

To a certain point, we are products of our environments, personalities, and experiences. Case in point, I can only write this book from my perspective, my upbringing, and my life experiences. I am not so arrogant or naive to think that my way is the only way. However, I can say that, based on my life experiences, a certain approach is the best way for me. That does not mean that I can't learn something from others. That is the constant growing and evolving that I keep mentioning.

If you close your mind to all things contrary to your beliefs, how will you ever grow? There is something to be learned from just about everyone you will ever meet, some of it positive and some negative, some things to emulate and some to avoid at all costs.

We don't have to agree with one another's points of view. However, we do need to show one another mutual respect even if we don't agree with others' way of thinking. You are free to think how you want, and others are free to think how they want. Although you may think you are perfect and the world would be a much better place if everyone just thought like you and embraced your same ideologies, millions of people would totally disagree with everything you believe in or stand for. Does that mean you are wrong? No, it means that you think differently than them. Your way of thinking and that of another may be so fundamentally different that the best course of action is to choose not to associate with each other. Also, when the way you think is pushed onto others, that alone could cause them to think unfavorably of you. It's not necessarily about who's right or wrong; it's more about agreeing to disagree and not trying to force our views on everyone else.

That is a major problem in today's society. A particular group gets to voice its opinion. However, if someone does not agree with that point of view, he is given titles like sexist, racist, homophobic, or a host of other unflattering names. Young men, the rights that allow you to have an opinion are the same rights given to others to think contrarily to you.

I will ask you to keep an open mind to new things and not automatically shut them out simply because they are different. There is much to learn from those who think differently than you. Think about how boring it would be if everyone thought the same way. For example, I can't understand why everyone is not a Raiders fan. However, there are fans of thirty-one other National Football League teams who feel the same way I do about their favorite teams. It is their choice. However, when Raider and Bronco fans start beating on one another just because they cheer for opposite teams, that is taking it too far. Of course, this example is made in fun, but the concept and sentiment are very real.

Here is a more serious example: Just in case you haven't noticed, I am a Christian, a follower of Christ. I believe that Jesus is the Son of God, He died on the cross for our sins, and He rose from the dead three days later. When I die in this flesh, I will be with Him in heaven for eternity. I know that everybody does not share the same belief as I have, and that is okay. Just as I was free to make my choice to follow him, everyone else is free to make their choice as well. However, for me, there is no other way. If you had known me back in the day, you would know that I have not always thought or lived my life as I do now. The important point is that my lifestyle and faith belief are my choices. I respect the freedom of choice for others even though they may differ from mine.

I am not fond of people telling me how to think, and that is exactly what happened when I chose to follow Christ. I went to a church that would beat people over the head with the Bible (figuratively speaking). They were told that if they didn't accept Christ right that minute, they were going straight to hell. While that did get my attention, it was the God that loved me enough to sacrifice his son so I didn't ever have to be separated from him that closed the deal for me.

Some may think I'm crazy for my beliefs, just as I think it is scary how people can live without Him. It's not my job to beat anyone over the head with my beliefs. It is my responsibility to share the message and let you choose for yourself.

On this journey, young men, you will encounter people with opposing views, including on religion, politics, race, cultures, sexual preference, and much more. Just because you don't agree does not give you the right to act in a disrespectful manner. Choose your views based on your own independent, intelligent thought and not that of a particular group or crowd.

Several years ago when I was a special agent in the Bay Area, I was working with my unit in an undercover capacity in a crowd of protestors in front of San Quentin State Prison. The crowd was predominately antideath penalty and was protesting that an inmate on death row was going to be executed at midnight.

Most of the time, the protesters would protest calmly with banners, signs, chants, and candles. However, on this one occasion, this one man who was very pro-death penalty was in the crowd, and he was making his position known as well. This normally passive group of anti-death penalty people suddenly became very aggressive and hostile toward the man. Things got so bad that we had to step in and calm everybody down.

During this event I remember thinking that the same rights that allowed the anti-death penalty protestors to make their views known are the exact same rights that allowed the pro-death penalty man to voice his views. The pro-death penalty man was not loud or boisterous; he simply carried a sign that clearly depicted his views. The anti-death penalty crowd became hostile solely because his opinion was contrary to theirs. So are we saying people get to have rights to voice their opinion, but only if that opinion is the same as ours? That kind of thinking is a problem. You simply don't get physical with people just because their views are different than yours.

"Hatred stirs up conflict, but love covers all transgressions."
—Proverbs 10:12

Politics

The purpose of this section is not to tell you how to vote but to put in your mind the importance of voting now or when you are of age. Several chapters back, we were discussing the importance of education and how our ancestors fought, bled, and died just for us to be allowed to read and go to school. The same is true for the right to vote. Our people paid a high price—some with their lives—for us to be able to vote. The least we can do as a form of gratitude for their sacrifice is to get off our butts, go to the polls, and cast our votes.

I won't give you a history lesson on the sacrifices made on our behalf, but I will say that we as a people have a responsibility to let our voices be heard by voting, not only for the president every four years but at the local and state level as well. One of the lame excuses I hear from people of all ages for not voting is, "I am just one person, so it's not going to make a difference anyway." I'm sorry, but that is nothing but a weak excuse for not carrying out your civic duty.

Yes, you are only one person, but it's not just you; it is a collective voice. It includes the voices of those brave individuals who dared step past men with white sheets on their heads to cast one vote. It's the voices of the individuals who were beaten and hung from trees because they desired the rights many of us have today. For those reasons alone, I don't do mail-in voting; I show my face at the polls. That's my way of showing my appreciation for the sacrifices made to allow me to do so.

Young men, I don't care if no one in your family has ever voted. Change has to start with someone, so let's make that someone you. This book is not about being males; it's about being men—men of character, leaders not just followers. This book is about your individual accountability, your responsibility to do the right thing. I don't care what everyone is *not* doing; I care about what you are going to do and what kind of man are you going to be.

Vote, vote, and vote—I don't care if you choose to be a Democrat, an independent, or a Republican; I just want you to know the difference for yourself. Like everything else we have been talking about in this book, make an informed decision based on what you know for yourself, not what someone else has told you. I don't want you to be a blind follower in anything in life.

When you do vote, do so with knowledge. Take the time to know the issues and the candidates for yourself. Pay attention to the news and read up on the pressing issues. Know what's going on around you. While there are indeed many things wrong in our political system, pay a little attention to what's going on in the world as well. Millions of people are oppressed in nations led by dictators. People are dying daily for the right that many in our nation take for granted. Without a doubt, our nation is far from perfect, but trust me—there are much worse places in the world.

Another way to voice your concerns in addition to voting is by protesting issues that you feel are unfair. Protesting in a nonviolent manner is one way and is very much the American way. However, when a protest turns into looting and the burning of your own neighborhood, it becomes more of a detriment than an asset to any cause.

Burning, looting, and other extreme acts of senseless violence distract from the initial issues and open the door for criminal opportunists to take away from the matter at hand. I feel this way because of the period in which I was born and my profound respect for Dr. Martin Luther King Jr. Of course, people were angry at the lack of social equality during Dr. King's short-lived time as our leader. However, he knew that the changes needed in our nation were not going to come from looting, burning, and senseless violence.

Many years ago when I still lived in Stockton, I somehow got into a politically motivated conversation with a much older white man at the gym. I can't remember exactly what was said, but I will never forget his response to something that apparently impressed him. His response was something along the lines of "You're not like most blacks," because I spoke well. I am sure that's not exactly how he said it, but that was the basic context. This man was probably around seventy-five years old. I am sure he had good intentions and thought he was giving me a very sincere compliment.

I remember just looking at him to see if he was serious, which he surely was. I didn't act a fool because it would have served no purpose. His ignorance was blinding him to the fact that his statement was offensive on many levels. However, it did serve as a reminder that there are still people out there that believe we as a people are not capable of educated thought or the ability to speak intelligently. I am just one person, but I make sure that I represent myself, my family, and my people in a positive way every day. Know the issues and the candidates, and vote because people have died for you to have the right to do so.

> *"The integrity of the upright will guide them, but the crookedness of the treacherous will destroy them."*
> —*Proverbs: 11:3*

Racism

Moving along, let's talk a bit about another very popular and heated subject—racism. What is it, and does it still exist in today's America? So let me answer the existence question first since it is the easier one. The answer is a resounding, absolutely, without-a-doubt, "Yes, it still exists." I am sure that doesn't surprise anyone.

I would assume that the level of racism you experience probably depends on your present environment, either where you live or where you work. I am sure my experiences of being born and raised in California are much different than someone raised in the South. While our stories may be different, the damaging effects of it racism are not minimized.

I have yet to visit places like Mississippi or Alabama. However, I have been to Atlanta, Georgia; Memphis, Tennessee; Louisville, Kentucky; and New Orleans, Louisiana. As far as I could tell from my relatively short visits, the races tend to be separated along social and economic lines. Also, the places I mentioned are the bigger cities in those states. I am sure there is even more racial division in the smaller towns. From what I saw and felt, there is certainly a different vibe in the Southern states. With that said, it does not mean that racism is found only in the South. It exists in California as well. However, depending on where you live in California determines how blatant and in your face the racism may be.

I spent many years as an investigator for the CDC, and during that time the job took me throughout California—from the top of the state at Pelican Bay State Prison to the bottom of the state at Richard J. Donovan State Prison in San Diego. I can tell you, things are not the same all over California. Those of you who think California is all sunshine and beaches, you are seriously misinformed. For example, parts of Northern California have mountains, giant trees, and snow in the winter. While working at places like Pelican Bay and High Desert State Prison in Susanville near Reno, Nevada, and numerous fire camps in the mountains searching for escapees, the only time I would see someone who looked like me was when I went to the prisons to interview inmates.

I will say that in all those years as an investigator, I personally never experienced any real issues because of my skin color. I mainly felt lonely on those trips and couldn't wait to get home. It may have been self-induced paranoia, but I didn't exactly get a warm and welcoming feeling in those places, so I tended to take care of all my business in the daylight hours. I'm not saying those towns were racist. There simply weren't many people of color there. I guess the same could be said if a white investigator from the places I just mentioned had to conduct investigations in Richmond, Oakland, or South Central Los Angeles. I am sure he or she would feel pretty out of place as well. I guess that is a long answer to a not-so-simple question. Yes, racism is very much alive and well. Sometimes it is subtle, and sometimes it can be as obvious as the sun.

Racism is defined as "a belief or doctrine that inherent differences among the various human racial groups determine culturally, or individual achievement. Usually involving the idea that one's own race is superior and has the right to dominate others; or that a particular racial group is inferior to others. As well as hatred or intolerance of another race or other races." That's a long way of saying one group dislikes another simply because they are different than their own.

Whenever I think of racism, it saddens me as it reveals a huge character flaw in not only Americans but in humanity. I am sure there are thousands of books that have been written about the many reasons and causes of racism. However, I like to keep things simple. To me, racism is driven by fear, ignorance, hate, and an underlying need to feel superior to another group—fear and ignorance of what one does not understand. Hate is either taught or brought on by negative experiences. Some feel the need to place more value on their own existence by minimizing the value of another.

Early in my life, I admit that the very idea of someone having racist thoughts toward me concerned me greatly. The thought that someone could dislike me to the point of hate without even knowing me was hard for me to understand. It simply didn't make any sense to me at all. Prejudging and hating an entire race or even an individual without knowing anything other than the color of their skin is complete ignorance. Remember, ignorance is not necessarily stupidity; it is the lack of knowledge of a particular subject. I do believe, however, that ignorance can morph into stupidity. Racism is a result of ignorance. Racism is hateful and hurtful, and it does not make a difference which group does the hating. There are racists in all races— black, white, Hispanic, and Asian. Color lines do not define racism; it is still fueled by ignorance and fear.

Racism is blinding. It does not allow people to see the good in others due to superficial differences like skin color. Racism causes barriers that will not let us work together to overcome our perceived differences. I say *perceived differences* because, due to our blindness, racism will not allow us to see our similarities. Before we are black, white, brown, or whatever makes you different, we are human. Sure, we have different experiences, religious beliefs, cultures, and so on, but those alone should not be a reason to hate.

I have a sense of pity for people who are so blinded by their bigotry and hate that they can't see me for who I am. I am a very proud black man, but at the same time, I am more than simply the color of my skin. So I refuse to let their ignorance and hatred take away my energy and joy. If I match hate with hate, they have won and I forfeit my power to choose, and I refuse to allow that. I will associate with people based on things that really matter, like character, attitude, and moral behavior. I would have missed out on many wonderful relationships had I been blinded by hate and refused to associate with people solely because they were not black.

Unfortunately, racism has deep roots and a long history in this nation. White people need to understand that black people are not simply going to "get over" the horrors of slavery and its lasting effects on our culture. Black people, we cannot be naive regarding racism, but at the same time we need to understand that not all white people are racist. I refuse to believe that all of any group is bad because of the sins of some. When faced with racism, deal with it on a case-by-case basis. Also, every white person who does not get along with or like you personally is not necessarily a racist. Don't be so quick to drop the race card because once that card is dropped, it is not so easily picked up. All-consuming hate does nothing but blind and hurt the one doing the hating.

If not all then most black men in America have been touched by the ignorance of racism. I have been in line at an ATM after working out at the gym, and my mere presence scared this white lady so much that she walked away from the machine without taking her money. As she walked away, I asked her if she wanted "this" as I pointed to her money still in the machine. She couldn't get her money and leave fast enough. Her fear and ignorance would not even allow her to say thank you. She will never know that I would risk my safety to protect her, not because she deserved it but because I took an oath to serve and protect. All that lady knew was that a black guy in sweats was standing in line and she might get robbed.

On more than one occasion, I have been on the job working a case in an undercover capacity and been pulled over for nothing more than driving while black. I would be lying if I said incidents like these didn't bother me, but I refuse to allow the action of a few ignorant people (cops included) to fill my heart with hate.

There are some white people I don't like, but it has nothing to do with the color of their skin. It has to do with their being idiots. I know some idiotic black folks as well that I would go to great lengths to avoid. The bottom line is that you should let individual actions dictate your behavior toward people, not something as superficial as skin color. Food for thought—you call someone you don't know a racist and treat them differently based on nothing more than their skin color. However, when someone does the same thing to you, you become angry. Tell me, what is the difference between you and that person you are calling a racistis? Aren't you both acting in an ignorant manner? Hate is hate and blindness is blindness, despite the color of the skin.

> *"Every man's way is right in his own eyes, but the Lord weighs the heart."*
>
> —*Proverbs 21:2*

Crime

For most of this book we have been talking about the importance of making good choices, wise decisions, and facing the consequences when you don't. Not too many times in your life is that going to be more evident and necessary than when it comes time for you to make the decision between being a person who obeys the law or being a criminal.

You and only you can ultimately make that decision. You need to decide if the criminal life and its consequences are the road you want to travel. When we talked about being proactive in your life, the same concept applies here. Make the decision much sooner than later. When you do make the decision, you need to ensure that you come up with a plan to avoid that road. Things you need to consider in your plan include the type of people you associate with and the places you hang out. Being proactive in this plan means much more than just saying, "I am not going to be a criminal." You will need to include action that is consistent with that statement and avoid situations that can lead to negative consequences.

Make sure to put added emphasis on the consequences portion of the equation because that's what it all boils down to. Are the consequences, which can include spending your life behind bars or death, worth the money or fun you think you may be having? Only you can answer that question. If you decide to go down the crime road and end up in prison, please don't act shocked or dare ask yourself, *How did I end up here?* You need to be accountable for your actions, which means you know exactly how you ended up behind bars. It all started with you consistently making bad choices and decisions. Also, failure to give an advance thought about what direction you are going is a decision as well, so don't try that excuse either.

A minute ago, I mentioned the fun you might think you are having. I said that because most of the guys I grew up with who went down the road of crime didn't wake up one day and say, "Hey I think I want to be a criminal." It was their continued activity that led them in that direction. Some did choose the criminal life early on because that was what they saw around them; therefore, they didn't really put any real thought into the consequences of that continued activity.

The guys I knew who went down that road engaged in activities that evolved over time. It began as doing small things, and then it turned into things that got them arrested, sent to jail, and eventually prison. It usually starts with hanging out with the wrong people and then deciding that since everyone around you is drinking and doing drugs, you will do the same. Then it can grow into committing robberies, burglaries, gang banging, and selling drugs. After a while, it just becomes the norm, and committing crimes is the only life you know.

As a quick side note, I don't want it to appear that we're just flying right by the use of drugs and alcohol. While I don't have the numbers to support it, I would think it safe to say that the vast number of people locked up chose the wrong path while under the influence of drugs or alcohol or both. That's another choice that starts out as just having a good time but can evolve into the beast that is now making most of your bad decisions for you.

Making good choices and decisions is hard enough when you are 100 percent sober. Why in the heck should you make it that much harder by adding outside influences like drugs and alcohol to the mix? Young men, when I talk about drugs, I am also talking about marijuana. People tend to think there is nothing wrong with smoking weed, but I disagree. Anything that alters the way you think and possibly lead to more powerful sources of getting high just can't be a positive in your life.

Regarding the choice of heading down the road to crime and its consequences, it is not always the one big decision that gets you on your way but often a series of little ones that start the dominoes falling. It includes the failure to decide to stop yourself when you know you are heading in the wrong direction.

Not only do you have to make up your mind now, but everything you do needs to support that decision. You can't say you are not going down that road but continue to hang out with the people who live that lifestyle. You can't walk the straight line sometimes. You can't decide to make good decisions most of the time. In the area of crime and its consequences, all it takes is to get caught one time and your journey will be altered forever.

I made up my mind early on that I didn't want to be like my father if it meant that choice would put me behind bars. I am not ashamed to say it, but the consequence of going to prison scared the crap out of me. Whatever it takes for you not to choose that life—be it fear, loss of freedom, or the idea of being locked up with nothing but men all day every day—whatever keeps you from heading down that road, so be it.

Sometimes motivation comes from odd places. For me it took me seeing my father locked up to motivate me early on that a life of crime and its consequences were not for me. It took my seeing the person my stepfather was to motivate me not to be the same type of man he was. Find your own motivation and pursue that path with passion.

I cannot stress enough the importance of forward thinking, having a plan, and choosing the direction you desire your journey to go. You are going to have to be a leader even if it means being your own man and leading yourself. If you know something is not the right thing to do, then don't do it. If you see trouble in front of you, be like a ship at sea. When the captain sees a storm on the radar screen, he changes course immediately to go around the problem. Only a foolish person stays the course even when he knows trouble awaits him if he continues on his current path.

If you have to walk the straight path alone because all of your friends are heading down that wrong road, then that's just how it has to be. Only you are going to be held accountable for your decisions. Only you are going to have to face the consequences of your actions. I don't care how much money you are pulling in as a thug, I promise you it's not worth the consequences. I don't care how tight you think you and your boys are, no one is going to do your time for you when you end up in prison. If it takes working a minimum-wage job to stay out of prison, then again, so be it. The last thing a prison needs is another black man. Trust me when I say there is no shortage of black men in our prisons.

Here's another reason you need to be proactive in your life in regards to being a criminal. There are people in the world who expect for you to have a bunch of kids that you will never take care of. They also expect you to find your way to prison. Don't help make them right by making bad choices and decisions.

Earlier, we established that life is not fair and even less so when you are a black male. The reality is that if you are black and you get busted for a felony, chances are you'll do more time for the crime than if you were white. I'm not saying that is all the time, but I am saying it happens far too much.

So here's the thing: if you already know the deck is stacked against you, why play the game? We already know things are not always fair for the black man in our criminal justice system. Then why do we continue to test it? We have clearly concluded that the system has some serious flaws, but now what? The "now what" is self-accountability. Until the system can be more equal and fair, it is on you to control the things you can. You cannot control the criminal justice system, but you can control your own actions. If you don't commit a crime or put yourself in negative situations, your chances rise significantly in your favor of not getting caught up in an unfair system.

There are always exceptions. There indeed are people in prison for crimes they did not commit. However, most of the inmates I have come across over my career did do the crime they were convicted of. We can talk all day about how the system is unfair and I will totally agree with you. However, I will still say you have a better chance when you don't put yourself in that system in the first place. You can't control the system, so you had better control your actions to avoid it.

I equate "the system" to the big bully on the block, the one who beats down just about anybody who dares to walk down his block. So let's say you are walking down the street and you see the bully. However, instead of avoiding the bully, you decide to continue walking toward him. Then to make matters worse, you pick up a stick and hand it over to the bully to beat you over the head with it. I know that sounds silly, but so is putting yourself in an unfair system that is not meant for your success. The bully (the system) does not need your help (the stick). Stop giving the bully power over you by committing crimes.

I do understand that crime is considered an option by some who are unable to find work, but it is still a choice. There are those who think it is simply a lot easier to take something from someone than it is to work for it. We can make all the excuses we want, but like I said before, "The world does not care about your excuses."

Things are tough for a lot of people, including those who do not choose crime as an option. We need to be more accountable and stop making excuses. Be wise and make the right choices now because once you're in the system, most of your choices are made for you.

If you choose crime and go to prison, please don't play the victim role. The victim is the person whose home you broke into. The victim is the person you robbed of the money she worked hard to earn. The victim is the person you shot and his family who had to put him in the ground. You chose your path; therefore, you don't get to play the innocent victim card. It's still not fair, right? But you knew that when you decided to play the game. Guess what—it is also unfair to all the real victims who had no choice. There are millions of people who look just like you and me who choose to get up every day and go to work instead of choosing crime.

Speaking of choices, our ancestors had no choice when they were taken from their homes and families, put in chains, stored on ships like animals, and brought to this country to be slaves. Their freedom was taken from them. If you choose crime, you surrender your freedom; it is not taken from you.

Does our system suck sometimes? Yes, it sure does, but we need to stop making excuses for the crime in our communities. You need to be responsible and stop making it easy for the system to suck you in like a vacuum. If we keep making excuses for those who decide to make crime an option, we are in effect helping them. It is also a major slap in the face to all those hard-working people who choose not to go down that road.

Do you want a surefire way of not getting caught up in the system? Well, there isn't one, but you can significantly reduce your chances by not using or selling drugs; by not robbing people or breaking into their houses; by not stealing, carrying guns, or shooting people. I could go on, but I think you get the point.

Crime is out of control in our communities. It is being committed by us, on us. We are victimizing ourselves. True, the system is not helping, but it is we who are killing us far faster and more often than the guns of law enforcement. Black men are dying senselessly every single day. If you are looking for the system to save you, that's not going to happen anytime soon. So we better start by addressing our own issues, like our young men killing each other at such a staggering rate.

I admit that I don't have all the answers, but I do know that the lack of black men leading the way for future generations is not helping the matter. It starts with individuals making better choices for themselves and then collectively making better decisions that can help our communities in a positive way. I believe it starts with changing the way we think. We need to stop making excuses for bad decisions and start holding ourselves accountable to one another.

> *"The prudent sees the evil and hides himself, but the naive go on, and are punished for it."*
> —*Proverbs 22:3*

Gangs

Since we just spoke about crime, we might as well move right into gangs. During my high school days, there were plenty of gangs around Stockton; however, it was nowhere near as bad as it is now. The closest

I ever came to being in a gang was with a bunch of guys who called themselves the Afro-Flips. It wasn't a gang; it was just a few black and Filipino guys who were involved in some form of martial arts. All we ever really did was talk martial arts; hang out at football games, skating rinks, and house parties; and of course, chase girls. There was no secret handshake, gang sign, emblem, or official colors.

In my day, the only people who were really banging in Stockton were the Mexican guys who we called *vatos*. Since we all grew up together, I never saw any real gang-related issues. Most of our issues came from cross-town rival high schools when we tried to get at each other's girls. I did see a rise in Hispanic gang activity after the movie *Boulevard Nights* came out in the late seventies. It depicted Mexican gang culture in the Los Angeles area. Now that I think about it, we probably didn't even come up with Afro-Flips thing until after we saw another late seventies movie, *The Warriors*, which was about some crazy gang stuff in New York.

I left for the navy in 1982 and didn't return to Stockton until 1986. I distinctly remember seeing a growth in Stockton's gang culture around 1988, which was right around the time the movie *Colors* came out. The movie focused on the issues between the Bloods and the Crips in South Central Los Angeles. In fact, during the film's debut in Stockton, there was a fatal shooting of a patron who was standing in line waiting to see the movie. Since the shooter was wearing red (color associated with the Bloods) and the victim was wearing blue (Crips), it was determined to be a gang-related homicide.

You need to be very aware of and careful regarding the influence that media, movies, and music can have on you. Today's films, television, and some rap music can tend to glorify violence and the gang life mentality. The fast money, power, and women attracted to the "bad boy" types are highlighted, but not the costly consequences of that lifestyle, which leads to prisons and cemeteries.

The purpose of this section is to let you know that there is no positive future in the gang life. People join gangs for numerous reasons, to include influence, money, reputation, being a part of a substitute family, the perception of power, perceived respect, family tradition, and peer pressure. Regardless of the reasons, I can tell you from decades of related work experience that there is no future in it. All gang-life roads lead to loss of freedom and loss of life.

Regardless of what the gang tells you to entice you into joining, it comes down to the perception of power and money. Gang life is all about leaders and followers. Most gang members serve no greater purpose than to do the bidding of the few leaders, who are all about themselves. We talked a lot about leaders and followers in the last chapter. One purpose of that chapter was to help you to avoid gang-type affiliations, to get you to be your own man, to make your own decisions, and to be very careful about whom you choose to follow. We also talked about, if you do choose to follow someone, make sure they have your best interests in mind. If someone wants you to do things you know in your heart are wrong, like committing crimes, then don't do it. Anything for which the consequences can lead you to being locked up or in the morgue can't be in your best interest. Someone who cares about your well-being will not lead you on a self-destructive path.

Much earlier in this book, we talked about creating your identity. The sooner you determine the kind of man you want to be, the easier it will be for you to not search for an identity in a gang. That is why it is so important for you to establish your own identity—so nothing and no one can sway you into doing things you don't want to do.

Sometimes when you are young, your sense of wanting to belong makes the gang life seem like a strong temptation. If all of your friends are doing it and you continue to hang with them, chances are you will eventually go along to get along. Maybe you go along because you don't want to be considered a punk. Never forget, it takes much more courage to stand alone for what you know is right than it does to simply go along.

Know who you are (identity) and what your expectations are for yourself. Don't waver or compromise, and then you can resist the call of gang life or any other activity that is detrimental to you. Gang life is not one of self-identity or moral character. It is a collective group of individuals who are in search of an identity and who chose that lifestyle even if it destroys their communities.

Throughout my career, I have dealt extensively with gang members in prison and on the streets. I have talked with youngsters who have come to prison and have decided to believe what the gangs told them. I have also talked to older guys who have been locked up for years and who wised up and saw the light. They finally understood that the gang leaders are self-serving and don't give a damn about them. Unfortunately, by then, they had devoted most of their lives to a gang. It is a sad thing when their eyes are finally opened and they see the gang life for what it really is. These men believed in the lie the gang was pushing. They thought they were serving as men of honor when in reality they were mere puppets for a select few.

The way things work in prison, or at least in California, is that if you are a member of a gang out on the streets, get arrested, and go to the county jail, your street gang politics will continue. However, once you get sentenced and sent to prison, all the street gang stuff goes away because at that point you fall under the politics and rules of the much bigger and more powerful prison gangs.

As an example, Southern California Hispanic gang members, with probably well over a hundred thousand members in the Los Angeles area alone, will fall under the strong arm of one of the most powerful prison gangs in California, the Mexican Mafia (EME). So if those individual street gang members had been warring with one another on the streets, all of that gets put away to serve the needs of the EME.

All of your gang activity is now dictated by the EME. You may have come to prison as a member of influence within your street gang, but once you hit the prison yards, everything changes. Not only did you forfeit your freedom by going to prison, but you also lost the little individual decision making you had in the gang. You chose to be a gangster and go to prison; now you get to be told what to do and when to do it by the correctional staff and the gang.

You can always decline to do what the gang tells you, but just like everything else in life, there are consequences, and those for failing to comply with an order given by a prison gang are often severe and vicious. It's hard to see the love of the gang when they send two gangsters you thought where your homeboys to stab you in the shower or in your cell. You see why I try to get you to make good choices and decisions for yourself? While I gave the example of the Southern California Hispanic gangs, the same thing occurs for all races in all prisons. Nothing positive ever comes from being in a gang. Learn to make good choices and decisions or deal with the negative consequences.

I don't mean to try and scare you because I don't think that really works in the long term. I'm just trying to educate you so that you will make better decisions *now*. However, if the reality of the truth scares you as it did me, then that is fine too. I am for whatever it takes for you to be your own man and not be a part of a dictatorship-like gangs.

> *"My son, do not walk in the way with them. Keep your feet from their path. For their feet run to evil, and they hasten to shed blood."*
>
> —*Proverbs 1:15–16*

Dealing with Law Enforcement

Besides electing a new president, another major hot topic in the news across the nation is the multiple deaths of black men and women by law enforcement officers. These deaths have been the match that has ignited numerous incidents of civil unrest across the nation.

With the advanced technology of the internet and social media, news can travel across the country and the world in a matter of seconds. Also, with the same advances in social media comes the ability for all to instantaneously voice their opinions of immediate guilt or innocence in any circumstance.

Long before this became a national hot-button issue, the subject of dealing with law enforcement was the primary talking point during the Youth and the Law Forums hosted by the 100 Black Men of Sacramento, of which I have been honored to be a panelist for many years. The panel consists of black men from various law enforcement agencies, to include state and federal judges, police, sheriffs, probation officers, and corrections officers. We talk to the young men about issues related to the criminal justice system. We also focus heavily on how they need to conduct themselves when they have an encounter with law enforcement.

First and foremost, a law enforcement contact is all about safety for all involved parties. If you are stopped, even if you feel you haven't done anything, please make sure to keep in mind that your primary goal is to go home. I can tell you that is what the officer is thinking every day he or she leaves home to go to work.

It is important—and I cannot stress this enough—that you maintain your composure during a law enforcement encounter. Stay calm, completely comply with all orders given, and do not get an attitude. A negative attitude is not going to do anything but escalate the situation and make things worse. Some of you might ask why you have to stay calm when you didn't do anything wrong. The simple answer is because you want to live and not become a statistic. I am not saying you need to be all smiles and act like you enjoy getting "jacked" by the police for no reason that you are aware of. I told you, the first thing to think about is your safety and that your goal should be to go home. This is also a good time to remember that although you may feel you didn't do anything wrong, you are still accountable for your actions. So watch what you say and do during the encounter.

When you get stopped and detained by a law enforcement officer, you are no longer in full control. However, you are still in control of your attitude and actions. If you didn't do anything, chances are the contact will be nothing more than a major inconvenience and you will be on your way. You may be angry and highly agitated as you head home, but that is much better than being in jail or a coffin.

If you feel you were treated unfairly, get the officer's name and badge number, which should be visible on his or her uniform. Immediately document the encounter as soon as you are free to go. Other things to include in the documentation are the words and actions of the officer who you feel treated you in an unprofessional manner. Also, include the time of day, location, and possible witnesses. Clearly explain in detail the behavior you felt was unprofessional and uncalled for. Take the information you have written down and file a formal complaint with the officer's department. Do not be lazy and just make a phone call to complain. You can make a phone call in addition to the formal written complaint, but make sure the incident is written down and submitted.

Now, let's go back to getting the officer's name and badge number. If at all possible, be discreet about it by simply looking at his badge and name tag. Memorize the information and write it down as soon as you are released. In effect, you are writing the officer up, and there is no need to tell the officer of your intended action. Just get the information and do it.

If there is no visible badge number or name tag, then calmly ask the officer for his name. Do not get irate and tell the officer he'd better give you his "mother f-ing" name and badge number. Do not cuss at the officer at all, even if he is in the wrong. Remember, your whole goal is to go home and not end up on some accident report.

Keep copies of everything given to you when you fill out your complaint. Ask for a receipt that indicates your filing. In most cases, it will have a complaint number. When you leave, document for your own records the name and badge number of the person you filed the complaint with. Make sure to include the day and time you filed. After some time (a week or two), if you have not been contacted, call and ask for the status of your complaint. Follow up even if you think nothing is going to be done. The outcome may not be in your control, but at least you know you did what you could. Control the things you can and keep an eye out for everything else.

The key is that to be able to file a complaint—please read this carefully—*you need to be alive.* Sure, you could get a major attitude and talk about the officer and his mama, but all that does is escalate things and one thing leads to another. God forbid, an accident could occur, and you could end up dead. Your people will sue the department. The officer who shot you may or may not get fired or go to jail. However, none of that will mean anything to you because you will still be dead. Listen, young men, the last thing the community needs is another black man who died a senseless death because he couldn't be cool for a few minutes.

I know none of this sounds fair, but I made it clear long ago that this has nothing to do with fairness. We are talking about you getting through a tense encounter so you can be alive for your family. So control yourself in a situation that is outside of your control. Not using your head can get you hurt. Deal with the situation with wisdom, be smart, and comply with all directions given.

I am not taking this stand because I was a law enforcement officer but because I have been on both sides of these situations. As I previously mentioned, on more than one occasion while working in California's Bay Area and driving an undercover vehicle, I was stopped for nothing more than being black. I was at work doing my part to help keep the streets safe. Now if you don't think I was not boiling angry, you are sadly mistaken.

When those incidents happened to me, guess what I did? I pulled c as instructed, took a deep breath, gritted my teeth, and rolled down a' my tinted windows so the officer could clearly see me and the conten' my vehicle. I also put both hands on the steering wheel as I looked str? ahead, and I didn't say anything until the officer asked me a que (mostly because I was highly agitated, and when I am like that, the say, the better). I didn't make any moves until the officer instructed me, and that includes going for my wallet to show my identification and badge.

So as a law enforcement officer on the job, why did I need to do all that? Because I too don't want to wind up being on some accident report. I can address everything else later if need be, but making quick movements and getting in the officer's face is not the smart move at that moment. Like I said, first and foremost, I want to go home. I was not trying to be the next breaking news story. My wife, kids, and grandkids do not need to hear, "We are so sorry for your loss." So trust me—I know about unfairness too, but I would much rather be alive than make a point.

In a law enforcement encounter, if you got caught for something you did, or even if you did absolutely nothing wrong, remember to keep your attitude in check. Comply with all verbal orders, and do not make any sudden movements. If your hands are in your pocket, leave them there until told to bring them out. When you do bring them out, do it slowly and leave whatever is in your hands in your pocket. Do not bring your hands out of your pockets with anything in them. Again, you do not want to be an accident by letting the officer think you have a weapon in your hands. If driving, do like I did: roll down all the windows and keep your hands in plain view. Again, comply with all orders, and don't do anything until told to do so.

Now I give you these directions primarily regarding simple police contact in which you didn't commit a crime. In this type of situation, if you do what I told you, your chances of just being detained for a few minutes and being released to go home are very high. However, if you are out there committing crimes and carrying guns, you just significantly escalated your chances for bad things happening. Just like you don't want to be shot and killed, neither do the officers. I know because I have been on both sides of this fence. You hear about black men being shot and killed for nothing, and law enforcement officers hear and read on social media about their own being killed for nothing more than doing their job.

There are always two sides to any story, but there is only one truth. I was in law enforcement a long time. Most of that time, I was an investigator. I worked nearly five years in the Office of Internal Affairs (OIA), the unit that did the investigations into allegations of peace officer misconduct. As a result of these investigations, officers lost their jobs or went to jail, depending on the allegations. (This is why I stressed to you the importance of filing your complaints.) I say that to say this: I understand that there are indeed bad cops out there. I also know that the good ones far outnumber the bad ones who forgot their purpose and no longer deserve the right to wear the badge and serve in the ranks of the good ones.

I too listen to the news and read the articles on social media. Without a doubt, we have major problems regarding some of these shootings. However, it is my opinion that the theory about the concerted effort by all law enforcement officers to wage war on all black men is not an accurate one.

The problem lies when we fail to look at each incident independently. They occur in different parts of the country, but we try to put them in one collective pot. It simply doesn't work like that. From experience, one of the biggest problems with law enforcement agencies working together has always been communication. Most agencies within a given county have problems due to radio communications and differences in policies and procedures. So the idea of thousands of agencies coming together to wage war simply isn't practical.

With today's speed of social media, it is too easy to clump all the incidents together. Each case is often separated by thousands of miles, is independent, and has its own individual set of circumstances. The same is true of the killings of law enforcement officers. Each case is separate and has its own case factors.

During my time with the OIA unit, my first assignment was as an original member of CDC's first Deadly Force Investigation Team (DFIT). It was our responsibility to investigate and review all officer-involved shootings inside and outside the prison that involved CDC staff. We would complete our investigations and submit a report of fact to the local district attorney of the affected county. I can tell you those officer-involved investigations are very complex, extremely time-consuming, and never as cut-and-dried as they initially appear. The biggest issue in these investigations is that they involve people, including the shooter, victim, and witnesses, all of whom have different perspectives and viewpoints.

As an investigator for most of my career, my job was to be a finder of fact and search out the truth based on those facts. Unfortunately, not everyone is as honest and truthful as we would like them to be. That includes officers and victims. Sometimes, what may appear to be a lie is nothing more than that individual's perception at that time. You have to remember that these are all extremely intense, stressful, and critical incidents; therefore, clear thought is not always present. I personally took great pride in being a fair investigator. I let the facts lead me where they may. I always conducted an investigation the way I would like to have it done if it I were being investigated.

I am retired now, but that doesn't mean my investigative eyes have closed; I did it too long, and it is just a part of who I am. When I see videos of some of these shootings, I look at them from an objective viewpoint, remembering that I only see what is being shown and don't have all the facts. With that said, I have to admit that some of the videos do concern me, without a doubt. With my limited knowledge of what took place in its entirety, some of the cases make me wonder what exactly the officer encountered that warranted the use of deadly force. If there is not much more than what is seen in the video, then the officer is going to have some serious explaining to do. The officer must be held accountable for his or her actions if found guilty of a crime, just like any other citizen.

The way I see it, wrong is wrong regardless of whether you are civilian or a law enforcement officer. We all are responsible for our actions. Cases in which people who have a gun in their possession are being shot present their own set of circumstances. Once a gun is observed, the chances of a calm and peaceful resolution seriously decrease.

As I said, I do not believe there is a national collective war on black men, but some areas of the country do appear to be worse than others. Until the problems are addressed at the federal level, it is going to take aggressive action at the state and local levels. It is going to require law enforcement officers and the community to work together. There needs to be a mutual effort to build bridges and not create greater divides.

The community is going to have to understand that the job of the law enforcement officer is inherently dangerous and has unique challenges. The community also needs to understand that not every person who is shot is innocent, especially those out there carrying guns. We need to stop making martyrs out of people who were doing things they had no business doing. Not holding people accountable for their actions hurts us as whole. The consequences of carrying guns and pointing them at police are never good. With that said, not everybody who gets busted for crime deserves to get shot. That is why it is imperative to look at each case individually and objectively and let the facts speak for themselves.

Law enforcement as a whole has to do a better job of incorporating diversity training. They need to stress the fact that not all black men are criminals, nor do they all pose an immediate threat regardless of what side of town they live on. Law enforcement officers also need to understand the perception that the public has when it is determined that a black man was killed unjustly and nothing appears to happen to the officer. Justice needs to be equally served, just as when a law enforcement officer is killed in the line of duty.

One of the biggest problems with interaction between most black communities and law enforcement officers is the lack of communication. A lack of communication and understanding of the other leads to mistrust. I believe this divide could at least be partially bridged if more blacks in our communities would work in law enforcement in the communities they came from.

Sometimes the miscommunication simply comes from not understanding the wants and needs of one another. You could have a white officer take a job in a city and get assigned to a predominantly black area. The chances are that the officer may not have ever been around people of color and may not understand the differences in culture. If the officer is not mature or secure within himself, he may attempt to cover his deficiencies with excessive flaunting of authority. The same could be said of those in our communities. The only time they see a white person is when someone is going to jail or worse. We need something to bridge these gaps. People fear and distrust things they don't understand.

More black law enforcement officers could help in many ways—one being they would have a deep-rooted connection to the communities in which they serve, which adds commitment for it to thrive and succeed. More black officers can help minimize issues that arise from the lack of understanding and communication. Black officers can serve as a bridge to educate white officers on how things really work within the black community, and they can also help the community better understand the role of law enforcement.

From my experience inside the prison and on the streets of predominantly black areas like Richmond and Oakland, I have seen how cultures can clash and escalate already tense encounters. On the inside and outside, I have witnessed situations in which white officers failed to understand that wearing a badge does not give you the right to speak to people any way you want. I have noticed that even when people are being arrested, if you treat them in a professional, respectful manner, situations have a better chance of going more smoothly than if you use the heavy-handed "you better do what I say because I'm the police" method.

I have witnessed numerous situations in which the lack of understanding of cultural differences and a feeling of disrespect have escalated rather small situations into full-scale incidents. In prison, a black inmate is instructed to do something by an officer, but the message is perceived as negative and disrespectful. The inmate knows and understands his present incarcerated state, and he ultimately knows he must comply with orders. However, if he doesn't feel the disrespect is warranted, he will let the officer know it. The officer has to understand that an individual who has lost his freedom often feels the only thing he has left is his self-respect. But often, the officer sees the inmate's voicing his disapproval of the perceived disrespect as insubordination, and the situation quickly escalates from a verbal matter to a physical one. The underlying problem is the lack of understanding of each other. The officer does not understand that just because the individual is an inmate, he cannot speak to him in a disrespectful manner. The inmate feels he is only voicing his disapproval of the perceived disrespect. However, the officer is interpreting the manner in which the inmate is voicing his displeasure as aggressive hostility.

On the streets, I have seen law enforcement officers in a heightened adrenaline state during an arrest or serving a search warrant treating others in the residence as if they had done something wrong because they just happened to have a relative who is wanted for something. When Mom or

Grandma voices her disapproval of what she feels is disrespect in her own home, the officer perceives her disapproval as aggression and interference to the officer trying to do his job. Mom and Grandma have to understand that the service of such warrants can be extremely dangerous situations, and the officer's aggression may be a result of the added stress of the situation. The officers, in turn, have to understand that while the situation may indeed be stressful, they need to watch what they say and how they say it. They also need to remember that not everybody in the home is a criminal. All that Mom and Grandma know is that the police have just burst into their home pointing guns and doing a lot of yelling. No matter who you are, that would be upsetting.

I have seen variations of both of these scenarios on many occasions and have been able to defuse some of them by my presence and understanding of the present cultural dynamics. Black law enforcement officers have a unique ability and responsibility to try and help bridge this gap. There are times when no amount of understanding or communication is going to stop a situation from escalating. During these situations, the officers—black and white—have jobs to do, and that is to maintain safety for the public and other officers.

As a black law enforcement officer, I always took it upon myself to act as that buffer. I've been told I could be a bit of a hard butt (for the record, I call it being firm and consistent), but I am also fair. The right thing for one is the right thing for all. Now if a person's actions required arrest or the use of force, I was going to do my job. However, I promise you that if I was around, force would be used because of the person's actions, not because of the color of his or her skin.

The addition of black officers has to be nurtured and fostered by the community as well as embraced by law enforcement in general. What I mean by that is that instead of calling black law enforcement officers "Uncle Toms," we need to give them support and be thankful they are representing our people in a positive light. If as a young child all I ever heard and saw was negativity directed toward black law enforcement officers, I wouldn't want to grow up to be one. The end result is that this mentality makes it nearly impossible to get black kids to grow up and want to serve and protect their own communities.

Just as criminals hate law enforcement on the streets, the same feeling carries on inside of prison. I remember a situation that occurred when I first started working at the prison. Something happened that required additional assistance from officers. As I was responding to the incident, I heard one young black inmate say, "Check out this Uncle Tom." I was brand new and was caught off guard by his statement. As time went on, I realized that some black inmates had added resentment toward black officers. I later learned that the added resentment came mostly from the younger inmates. However, on the flip side, older black inmates who had been around a while would tell me, "Dangerfield, don't trip on the younger dudes. I am glad you are here. I remember how things were when the only black skin I saw was on inmates." So when you are giving a black officer grief for trying to represent our community, please take a moment to think how it would be if none of us wore a uniform.

So in closing this subject, I will say there are no easy solutions. I just know that we have come far, but the racial injustice matter is far from being resolved. However, we definitely cannot afford to go backward. Until we get where we need to as a nation, I want you young men to pay close attention to the things we discussed in this section. Be smart, and don't put yourself in negative situations. However, if you find yourself in a bad spot, be smart by not making it worse by your attitude or actions. Remember to stay in control of yourself.

> *"My son, let them not vanish from your sight; keep sound wisdom and discretion."*
> —*Proverbs 3:21*

Prison

The previous few sections dealt with crime, gangs, and law enforcement, so now let's move on and talk about prison. We have talked plenty about how, in one way or another, prison has been connected to my life story for just about as long as I can remember, whether it was visiting my father in Folsom; the fear of going there myself, which directed the path of my journey; or my working with CDC for nearly three decades. Unfortunately, the connection with prisons in some form or another is all too familiar in our communities across the nation.

Somehow, we have to find a way to get it across to you young men that going to prison should not be normal. That it is not a natural life event, nor is it a rite of passage for men of color. We as a community have seen this vicious cycle for generations in some families, from grandfathers, fathers, and sons. Folks, this is not normal. We should not get so desensitized that we think, *That's just how it is where I come from.*

We have talked about the domino effect it has on our communities, ranging from black women being forced to raise our children without physical, emotional, or financial assistance from fathers who are doing time to our young men who are out there trying to figure things out on their own.

The issue of black mass incarceration has no easy solution as it is not only deeply woven into our communities, but there are certain parts of our nation and people who simply think prison is the natural path for our young men. There is still a need to continue to fight for equality in the legal system to include fair sentences across the board. If you commit a particular crime, the sentencing should be the same regardless of race or social and economic status. Many people have voiced this very thing for decades. Voices will continue to ring out on the injustice, and the fight will continue.

Until we as a nation make serious changes, what can we do in our own communities to help ourselves? I am a very big believer that change starts from within, and it begins with the way we think. Nothing changes until we as individuals, as families, and as a community change the way we think. We cannot afford to focus all of our attention on the clear and present fact that things are unfair for the black man. I believe we all agree that is pretty much a known fact. That fight will continue, but what do we do in the meantime? I believe we need to teach, preach, and demonstrate by example more self-accountability to our youth.

We need more accountability for actions and less excuse making. We still must prepare our youth for the unfairness that is bound to come. However, we cannot stop at the unfairness; we must also prepare them for how to navigate the waters of unfairness, how not to help life beat them over the head with the stick we give them.

Believe me, I know there is nothing easy about our dilemma, but I also know that nothing ever changes by our just talking about it. We can change the way we think and still understand there is no broad brush that is going to magically change things for the black man in this country anytime soon. I don't care how much a politician promises to make things better for us if we just vote for him or her. What happens once they get voted in? They seem to forget their promises and move on to their more-pressing agenda items—that is, until it is time for us to vote again, either for them or someone just like them. Meanwhile, the cycle continues: they promise, injustice continues, we vote them in, injustice continues. They forget their promises, and injustice continues. We forget their broken promises or outright lies, we vote them in again, and injustice continues.

While politicians are making promises, we are making excuses and our young men are still filling up our prisons at a mind-blowing rate. In addition to the fight for equality, our focus also needs to be on teaching accountability and on making better life choices and decisions to help avoid the negative consequences. We need to reinforce the concept of controlling the things you can. We know the system is unfair, so why would we purposely continue to put ourselves out there through negative behavior?

Committing crime is a choice, so let's stop making excuses for poor decisions. While we do have many black men locked up in prisons across this nation, we also have many more who have made the choice to not commit crimes. Is it not hard and unfair for all the brothers and sisters out here doing the right thing? These are choices and decisions made by both parties.

We have to change the way we think. If you think you are a victim, you are certainly going to be one. We have to stop making it easy for a well-known unfair system to beat us down. You can do everything right and still get sucked into the unfair system, but you increase your chances of unfairness tremendously when you commit crimes. Like I said previously in this chapter, "The last thing we need are more black men in prison." As long as we continue to help the system, more and more prisons will continue to be built.

The first prison in California was San Quentin, which was established in 1852. It was followed by Folsom in 1880. When I started working for the CDC in 1987 at Deuel Vocational Institution, which was built in 1953, there were only around fifteen state prisons open in California. By the time I retired in 2015, that number had more than doubled. That is not counting inmate fire camps and private prisons being paid to house California inmates in other states. Even with all that growth, California continues to struggle with overcrowding. During the last few years, CDC and the State of California have been trying to find ways to focus more on rehabilitation as a means to slow down the growing numbers. I think as a state, and perhaps as a nation, we are forced to move away from the "lock them up and forget about them" mentality.

When I talk to young men about prisons, I try to do it from more of a factual viewpoint rather than use the "scare them straight" approach. I do that because, while there is an initial fear factor, it will soon wear off after they leave our discussion. However, I drop real seeds of knowledge and let them come to a conclusion for themselves that prison just might not be the best route for them.

I always tell them there is nothing remotely cool about the loss of your freedom and being forced to live in cells. There is definitely nothing cool about being searched any time of the day or night. And sure as heck there is nothing even kind of cool about being searched butt naked to see if something is hidden in your body cavities. I tell them about the never-ending feeling of negativity and the constant stress that you learn to think is commonplace. I tell them about the constant threat of violence, the reality of predators and prey. I tell them about men using other men as women against their will. I tell them about the total loss of any real privacy, which includes not even being able to go to the bathroom alone and having to lie on your bunk and try to eat your lunch as your cellmate takes care of his bodily functions. I tell them about the reality of boys going to prison, not youth camps, as early as sixteen years old if their crimes are bad enough. At sixteen, you should be in high school, not locked up with some of society's fiercest predators. I tell them about the presence of pure evil and people who are completely without compassion. I also tell them about the kind of evil that will take your manhood and your life, shove you under the bunk, and eat your lunch as they wait for staff to realize that something's wrong.

I share a few stories from when I first truly realized I was working in a prison. I vividly remember when I was only three months in at most, and there was some serious commotion in the corridor. When an alarm sounded and the red light turned on, all inmates were required to "get on the wall," which meant they needed to get out of the way as staff responded to the location of the alarm. During this particular incident, not only did the red light come on, but a yellow light was illuminated, which I had never seen before. I soon found out that this light meant staff were to get all inmates out of the corridor to make way for the motorized gurney. So as the officers started putting inmates in housing units, which are right off the corridor, not knowing any better I found myself locked in a housing unit along with inmates. Within a few minutes, I saw a man being transported on the gurney with what looked to me like a shortened sword sticking out of his chest. In my entire career, it was the biggest inmate-made weapon I ever saw, and I saw a lot of them. At that very moment, things got real for me. I distinctly remember asking myself, *What the hell did I get myself into?* I thought, *There is no way someone can live with that thing sticking out of their body.* Of course, I was right—the man died.

Not everyone who goes to prison gets raped or stabbed, but plenty do. Prison does indeed change people. No staff member or inmate is ever the same person he was when he first went into that place. The world on the outside and the world on the inside are nowhere near the same. If you are doing things that can lead you there, then I suggest you stop. If you are not doing things that can get you there, then don't start. The bottom line is that it is your choice not to head down that road. Trust me when I tell you that there are much better decisions that you can make. It really is all about choices, decisions, and consequences.

> *"Because they hated knowledge and did not choose the fear of the LORD. They would not accept my counsel; they spurned all my reproof. So they shall eat of the fruit of their own way and be satiated with their own devices."*
> —*Proverbs 1:29–31*

CHAPTER 10

FINAL REFLECTIONS

Okay, young men, we are winding this thing down. I remember when I first dared to think about writing this book. I worried about and doubted many different things. However, as we get to the end, I realize that those worries and doubts were just excuses not to do what was in my heart, excuses not to share my knowledge and experiences with you. I worried about silly things like, *Who am I to dare even think about writing a book? Do I have enough information to fill a book?* Things like that will pop into your mind to get you to doubt yourself and stop you from carrying out your purpose. This journey is ongoing, and it never ends until your heart stops and you stop breathing. We should always be in various states of enlightenment and growth. Don't try to stifle the process; embrace it and expand your horizons.

When I started the actual writing process, my mind was flooded with many memories. Some were good, and some were not so good, yet they all went into the making of me, my identity, and my character. This book forced me to think about things I had either forgotten or tried to forget.

This book reinforced what I have believed for some time now, and that is that my life, talents, gifts, and abilities are not for me alone. That also includes my mistakes and the hard lessons I have learned along the way. This book has provided me with a way to give back by sharing my triumphs, achievements, failures, and other less-than-stellar life moments to help you.

Some of the periods in my life were filled with extremely difficult and dark times. Sometimes those situations were more than I thought I could bear. However, during those times, God guided and often carried me when I didn't think I could take another step. This book reminded me that no matter how dark it may get, don't ever quit whatever you do. Someone, somewhere, has it far worse than you. When the long term looks too bleak, slow it down and achieve little victories one day at a time.

Young men, please know that you come from proud, strong, and resilient people. Our ancestors endured lives much harder than we could ever imagine. Negativity will tell you that there is nothing good in you or in your life, but I am here to tell you that is a lie. Don't you dare believe that mess. However, it is up to you to nurture the positive and show everyone who doubted you just how wrong they were.

It's funny how I worried that I wouldn't have enough to say to fill the book. Apparently, I had plenty to say, and now I am having a hard time closing it out. Every day as I look at the news and see black boys killing other black boys, I feel loss—the loss for the victim, his family, and the community as well as the loss for the taker of life who will never fully know freedom again and whom he could have become had he made better choices and decisions in his life. It hurts my heart to see law enforcement officers taking the lives of our boys and men, justified or not. It hurts my heart to see law enforcement officers being killed at the hands of black boys and men. All lives do indeed matter, but it hurts my heart that we have to still remind people that "all" includes black lives as well.

When I see and hear about all of this senseless death, I can't but help wonder if maybe things would be different if we had more black fathers in our communities, more positive male role models leading, guiding, and teaching our boys by example. Sleeping around with a lot of different women and getting them pregnant doesn't make you a man. Making a lot of money selling drugs doesn't make you a man. Being big, strong, and able to knock people out because you think they "disrespected you" doesn't make you a man. Carrying a gun and pulling the trigger doesn't make you a man. What makes a man are the many things that we have already discussed throughout this book. Unfortunately, too many of our boys have misguided ideals of what a man is because there simply isn't one in their lives to teach and provide them with positive examples.

I am just one black man who decided to write and share my thoughts on another way of thinking and acting. It is not the only way. I am sure many people disagree with some things I have said, and that is okay. However, you made it to the last chapter, which means you have at least read the book. Since this is a book about making choices, it is now up to you to decide what you are going to do with it. Also, since you read the book, you no longer get to say no one ever cared enough about you to tell you there is another way.

Young men, life is indeed hard for black men. I would be doing you a disservice if I gave you nothing but a bunch of excuses to fail or, even worse, expected you to fail. I see more in you than a bunch of excuses. Our people need you to be men of character and self-accountability and to embrace the responsibility of being positive black role models that our communities are literally dying for you to be.

Earlier in this chapter, I mentioned that the writing of this book had awakened a lot of memories within me. It also stirred a lot of emotions as well. One of the most powerful emotions I have experienced is that of gratitude—to God for providing me with the experiences for this book, for the inspiration to write it, and for not giving me peace until I did. I am also thankful to those of you who have heard me out by reading this book and allowing me to be a part of your journey.

Some people may think our young people are lost and that writing this book is a waste of time because today's youth won't take the time to read it. I refuse to believe that. I fully understand that not all who read this will pay heed and learn the lessons that I have tried to share. However, I believe in my heart that some of you will learn something and will pass it on.

My Top Ten Beliefs and Thoughts

Of all the things we have discussed, I tried to summarize some in a top-ten list of things of which I could never sufficiently stress the importance. Since we discussed so many important subjects, I decided to make a list of the ones I wished someone would have told me as a boy and young man trying to find my own way. These are all things I had to learn so I could share them with you. I still use them to govern my life today.

1. Learn from your mistakes and those of others: I don't care who you are, you are going to make mistakes in life. If anyone ever tells you they have never made a mistake, I'm not saying they are lying, but they are not being completely truthful with you or themselves. Not all mistakes are created equal. Some will simply bring you embarrassment, and some can get you locked up or dead. Learn from your mistakes, and prove you have learned the lesson by not repeating them. If someone's mistake didn't work for them, more than likely it won't work for you either.

2. Fatherhood is the ultimate leadership role: Being a father is so much more than getting a girl pregnant. Making a baby is easy. It only takes a few minutes. However, being a father is a lifetime position. When the time comes (if it has not already), please take the responsibility of being a father seriously. Treat it as if it is the most important job in the world because it is. Remember that you should set the tone for what a leader is in your child's mind. You do it by taking the time to teach and guide them in the way they should go. More importantly you do it by setting the example.

3. Knowledge without action (or wisdom) is meaningless: If you have all the education and knowledge in the world but you don't put it to good use, what real purpose does it serve? Knowing the right thing to do and doing the right thing are not the same thing. If you know it's not the right thing to do, then don't do it. As my mom says, "You must wise up to rise up."

4. Be proactive, not just reactive: Taking life as it comes is a reactive mind-set. You may not be able to control all things, but that is no excuse for not being proactive in your own life. Have a plan and put that plan into action. When things happen that are contrary to your plan, then improvise, adapt, and overcome as you continue to push forward.

5. Control your anger: Know your hot buttons and learn to control them before the anger controls you. Remember, "I did it because I was angry" is not an acceptable reason for negative behavior.

6. Your actions speak much louder than your words: In the end, it is your actions (what you do) that define who you really are. It's not the smooth words or the empty promises that will be remembered. You could say absolutely nothing but do the right thing, and you will be remembered for being a man of action. Being a man of action is far better than simply being known as the guy who talked a lot but did very little.

7. It is all about accountability: To be the man I know you can be, you must hold yourself accountable for your actions instead of spewing empty excuses for not doing the right thing. We can always come up with grand excuses for our actions, but they do not outweigh our accountability for making better choices.

8. Character identifies the man: All men are different. We all have our own strengths and weaknesses. It is up to us to use our strengths for positive purposes. We must identify and face our imperfections so we can alter the things that hinder our growth. We decide what our identity is to be and the character traits we will need to become the men we desire to be.

9. In the end, it is the relationships that matter the most: The older I get, the more I understand just how true this concept is. Just as we are born, there will be a day when we will die. As you take your last breath, I seriously doubt your final thoughts will be about the stuff you owned or planned to own. As I live this life and embrace the truth of it being about much more than just about me, the more I want to know that my presence on this planet made a positive impression in the life of someone. What could matter more than making a difference in the life of another in a positive way? Material things perish, but making a positive impact in the life of others is what a legacy really is all about.

10. Choices, decisions, and consequences: If you forget everything in this book, please, please, please remember the equation, Poor Choices (PC)+Bad Decisions (BC)=Negative Consequences (NC). Be very careful with the choices you have and the decisions you make, and always strongly consider the possible consequences. If you don't like the potential consequences, then ensure that you make better decisions. If you want to succeed in this life, it is imperative that you think before you act. If you reverse it and act first, then it is too late and it will certainly lead to negative consequences.

I truly hope you possess your own copy of this book and will use it as a resource as you continue on your journey. Depending on what stage you are presently in on your journey, I am sure some of this book was foreign to you. Trust me and reread it again down the road; it will get much clearer as you grow.

I know you didn't think you were going to get away without one last story, did you? I didn't create this story, but it definitely relays the point I desire to make. One day a man was walking along the boardwalk, and he noticed people gazing intently at the beach's waterline. He started to walk through the sand toward the water. As he got closer, he saw what was capturing the people's attention. He saw that thousands of starfish had washed up on the beach. The man also noticed a young boy feverishly picking up and throwing the starfish back into the water one at a time. The man reached down out of concern for the boy, tapped his shoulder lightly, and said to him, "Son, please stop. There is nothing you can do to save all these starfish." The boy looked up at the man and calmly responded, "Perhaps that may be true, sir, but it's going to matter to this one," as he gently tossed the starfish in his hand back into the water. That is how change begins, one mind and heart at a time. Safe travels, men.

Last, here is a bonus to my top-ten list: Without Jesus in my life, none of the ten mean anything. Every man must choose his own path, and mine is the one paved by the sacrifice of Christ. The door is wide open for any who wish to enter.

> *"Behold, I stand at the door and knock; if anyone hears My voice and opens the door, I will come in to him and will dine with him, and he with Me."*
> —*Revelations 3:20*